MOSAIC II
A Listening/Speaking Skills Book

2nd presentation 3 mins. [Q - A]

HOME WORK

5/7   PP. 74 → 76 vocab

        PP 93 - 96 vocab

5/12   PP 114 - 115

        study PP 123 - 125

5/16   p. 131 vocab.

        PP 140 - 143 study expressions & conversations

5/19   PP. 3 - 4   Vocab.

        PP. 8 - 9 conversation practice

5/26   PP 156 - 158

MOSAIC II
A Listening/Speaking Skills Book

Jami Ferrer
Goleta Union High School District

Elizabeth Whalley
California Polytechnic
State University, Pomona

with contributions by:

Steven Carlson

Marilyn Bernstein

Steven Marx

Steven Hollander

William G. Carter

RANDOM HOUSE NEW YORK

This book was developed for Random House by Eirik Børve, Inc.

First Edition

9 8 7 6 5 4 3 2 1

Library of Congress Cataloging in Publication Data

Ferrer, Jami, 1947–
  Mosaic 2, a listening/speaking skills book.

   "Developed for Random House by Eirik Børve, Inc."
   1. English language—Text-books for foreign speakers.
2. English language—Conversation and phrase books.
I. Whalley, Elizabeth.   II. Eirik Børve, Inc.   III. Title.
IV. Title: Mosaic two, a listening/speaking skills book.
PE1128.F4262   1985   428.3′4   85–1815
ISBN 0–394–33726–3 (pbk.)

Manufactured in the United States of America

Text design: Janet Bollow
Cover design: Cheryl Carrington
Cover photograph: Peter Menzel
Photo research: Stuart Kenter
Technical art: Brenda Booth
Composition: Dharma Press

PHOTO CREDITS

CONTENTS

Preface   xiii

CHAPTER 1

LANGUAGE AND LEARNING   1

Lecture: To School or Not to School

Part One   2
Discussion   2
Vocabulary   3
Part Two   4
Skill A: Listening for the Main Point   4
  Listen In   4
  Speak Out   5
Skill B: Requesting the Main Point   7
  Listen In   10
  Speak Out   10

CHAPTER 2

DANGER AND DARING   13

Lecture: Hooked on Thrills

Part One   14
Discussion   14
Vocabulary   15

Part Two   17
Skill A: Noting Specific Details   17
    Listen In   21
    Speak Out   22
Skill B: Saying "Yes" and "No"   22
    Listen In   25
    Speak Out   26

CHAPTER 3

MAN AND WOMAN   31

Lecture: Becoming a Man, Becoming a Woman

Part One   32
Discussion   32
Vocabulary   33
Part Two   35
Skill A: Abbreviating: When and How   35
    Listen In   38
    Speak Out   38
Skill B: Extending Congratulations and Condolences   39
    Listen In   42
    Speak Out   43

CHAPTER 4

MYSTERIES PAST AND PRESENT   45

Lecture: The Origins of Our Solar System

Part One   46
Discussion   46
Vocabulary   47
Part Two   50
Skill A: Using Illustrations in Note Taking   50
    Listen In   52
    Speak Out   54
Skill B: Admitting Lack of Knowledge About Something   55
    Listen In   56
    Speak Out   57

CHAPTER 5

TRANSITIONS 59

Lecture: Jacques' View of the Stages of Life

Part One 60
Discussion 60
Vocabulary 62
Part Two 63
Skill A: Understanding and Making Analogies 63
   Listen In 64
   Speak Out 66
Skill B: Making Negative Statements or Comments Politely 67
   Listen In 68
   Speak Out 70

CHAPTER 6

THE MIND 73

Lecture: Dreams and Reality

Part One 74
Discussion 74
Vocabulary 75
Part Two 77
Skill A: Listening for Comparisons and Contrasts 77
   Listen In 79
   Speak Out 81
Skill B: Expressing the Positive View 85
   Listen In 86
   Speak Out 88

CHAPTER 7

WORKING 91

Lecture: Japanese and American Systems of Management

Part One 92
Discussion 92

Vocabulary 93
Part Two 94
Skill A: Listening for Causes and Effects 94
    Listen In 96
    Speak Out 101
Skill B: Persuading and "Giving In" 102
    Listen In 106
    Speak Out 107

CHAPTER 8

ETHICAL QUESTIONS 111

Lecture: Organ Transplants: Ethical Issues

Part One 112
Discussion 112
Vocabulary 113
Part Two 115
Skill A: Cohesion and Reference 115
    Listen In 118
    Speak Out 122
Skill B: Keeping the Floor and Taking the Floor 123
    Listen In 125
    Speak Out 126

CHAPTER 9

THE ARTS 129

Lecture: The Changing Sounds of Rock and Roll

Part One 130
Discussion 130
Vocabulary 130
Part Two 132
Skill A: Distinguishing Between Fact and Opinion 132
    Listen In 133
    Speak Out 139
Skill B: Expressing Disbelief and Doubt 140
    Listen In 143
    Speak Out 144

CHAPTER 10
ENERGY AND MATTER 147

Lecture: Discovering the Laws of Nature

Part One	148
Discussion	148
Vocabulary	149
Part Two	151
Skill A: What to Do When You Understand Each Word and Still Don't Understand	151
Listen In	152
Speak Out	153
Skill B: Giving and Receiving Compliments	154
Listen In	158
Speak Out	159

CHAPTER 11
MEDICINE 161

Lecture: Laser Technology and Medicine

Part One	162
Discussion	162
Vocabulary	162
Part Two	164
Skill A: Predicting Exam Questions	164
Listen In	165
Speak Out	169
Skill B: Acquiescing and Expressing Reservations	170
Listen In	171
Speak Out	172

CHAPTER 12
THE FUTURE 173

Lecture: The World in the Year 2000

Part One	174
Discussion	174

CONTENTS

Vocabulary   175
Part Two   176
Skill A: Critical Thinking   176
  Listen In   178
  Speak Out   180
Skill B: Speculating About the Future
and Reminiscing About the Past   181
  Listen In   183
  Speak Out   185

PREFACE

MOSAIC: THE PROGRAM

Mosaic consists of eight texts plus two instructor's manuals for in-college or college-bound nonnative English students. *Mosaic I* is for intermediate to high-intermediate students, while *Mosaic II* is for high-intermediate to low-advanced students. Within each level, I and II, the books are carefully coordinated by theme, vocabulary, grammar structure, and, where possible, language functions. A chapter in one book corresponds to and reinforces material taught in the same chapter of the other three books at that level for a truly integrated, four-skills approach.

Each level, I and II, consists of four books plus an instructor's manual. In addition to *A Listening/Speaking Skills Book*, they include:

- *A Content-Based Grammar I, II:* Each grammar chapter relates to a specific theme, so the exercises focus on contexts and ideas. There is a wide variety of communicative, functional activities.

- *A Reading Skills Book I, II:* Selections in these books come from many sources, including newspapers, magazines, textbooks, and literature. The emphasis is on building reading and study skills; for example, skimming, scanning, determining the author's point of view, reading charts and graphs, guessing the meaning of new words from context, making inferences, outlining, and techniques for remembering what has been read.

- *A Content-Based Writing Book I, II:* These books provide students with short readings on the chapter themes and include many prewriting, revision, and vocabulary-building exercises. The books focus on the writing process, particularly on techniques for gathering ideas, such as "brainstorming" and "freewriting," and on using feedback to rewrite.

- *Instructor's Manual I, II:* These manuals provide instructions and guidelines for use of the books separately or in any combination to form a progam. For each of the core books, there is a separate section with teaching tips and other suggestions. The instructor's manuals also include sample tests.

MOSAIC:
A LISTENING/SPEAKING SKILLS BOOK

Mosaic II: A Listening/Speaking Skills Book is unique among listening/speaking materials currently available. Most focus on either listening or speaking and teach either study skills or language functions. This text teaches study skills *and* language functions, while maintaining a strong focus on both listening *and* speaking. Active listening activities based on short but realistic academic lectures and sample conversations provide comprehension practice, while a variety of natural speaking activities reinforce use in context of language functions.

Content of the sample lectures and conversations has been carefully chosen to appeal to the interests and needs of the students. The various study skills and language functions are thereby presented in a context of useful information. The comprehension and production activities have also been carefully designed for maximum appeal to students. However, no two classes are alike, so activities are geared toward personalizing the learning process by allowing for a great deal of flexibility. The activities can generally be modified to reflect such things as local information, current events, names of students, and students' personal interests and experiences; teachers are encouraged to personalize the material whenever possible to keep student motivation high.

The text consists of twelve chapters. One study skill and one language function are presented in each chapter. The presentation of the study skills and functions is unique in its thoroughness and comprehensibility. Explanations include numerous examples and various idiomatic expressions for each of the language functions. Also in each chapter is preparatory material in the form of an introductory paragraph, discussion items, a vocabulary exercise, and various photographs. These portions of the chapter help prepare the students for the lecture by familiarizing them with vocabulary, getting them to recall what they already know about the topic, and stimulating interest and further questions.

This text is accompanied by a cassette program that contains the lectures and sample conversations for each of the chapters plus some explanatory comments. The conversations are printed in the student text; the lectures are not. Both appear in the key to the tape program, available from the publisher.

General Teaching Suggestions

1. Read through an entire chapter and listen to the taped material for that chapter before teaching any portion of it.

2. The book is intended to facilitate maximum student participation. During speaking activities respond to student requests for help, but as much as possible allow students to interact without interruption unless there are misunderstandings or miscommunications. Keep notes, if you need to, and give feedback after students have completed an activity if you wish. You don't want students turning to you for a judgment after each sentence they utter.

3. To facilitate the various role-plays and other interactive activities, you will probably need to disinhibit yourself and the students to some degree. This is where you can really use the personal information you know about the students: what amuses them? what saddens them? what excites them? Plugging a few tidbits of personal information into an already relaxed and "safe" atmosphere can do wonders.

4. The exercises are designed to teach skills, not to test proficiency. But students will generally need to be reminded that it's all right to make errors; they are not expected to be competent at each task already, but, through the process of learning from errors, to *become* competent at the tasks.

5. This text provides more practice exercises and activities in each chapter than most teachers would be able to use in a week of class time. Thus, if you wish to do a chapter a week, you'll have to choose among the activities provided.

Chapter Organization and Specific Teaching Suggestions

Opening Photo   The opening photo can be used in combination with the chapter title for topic anticipation. Let students consider what could be included in the chapter given this particular photo. Or let the photo trigger whatever thoughts and discussion it might. About four to six minutes of discussion will be sufficient for most chapters, but you may want to spend a longer time if the discussion is particularly productive.

Introductory Paragraph   This paragraph focuses on the topic and provides a link between the chapter theme and content of the lecture. It can be assigned as homework, read silently or aloud in class, or perhaps read aloud by a student or the teacher with the students' books closed to provide additional listening comprehension practice.

Discussion   This section allows students to relate their own knowledge, background, and experience to the chapter topic. Rather than concentrating on what they don't know, they can focus on what they do know about the topic, thus building confidence to tackle the lecture material. There are *no right or wrong answers,* of course, and students should be encouraged to share whatever they can. In the course of the discussions, you will get to know the students better, and they will get to know each other better. Most questions are open ended, and you will want to plan how much time to allow for the questions. Fifteen minutes or so are suggested. You may wish to select certain questions and do only those. Sometimes you may wish to have students write out the answers for homework. This will allow you to find out how your most reluctant speakers would have answered the questions and give all students additional practice expressing themselves in English.

Vocabulary   The vocabulary items are fundamental for understanding the lecture and useful for the students in other contexts as well. The vocabulary exercise may be assigned and done in class or as homework. Sometimes you may want students to work on these in groups to provide additional speaking practice. When pressed for time you can quickly read the correct answers to students and discuss only particular items that were problematic. Answers are in the instructor's manual.

Skill A   The study skills in this section are essential for academic success. An explanatory presentation is provided for each skill: the students should read this at home or in class before you discuss the skill with them. You might want to put key points on the board during the discussion.

Listen In, Skill A   Students listen to the lecture and do the accompanying listening exercise. You may want to follow the procedure described in the text for listening to the lecture, or you may choose your own procedure. For example, after the first listening you may have students listen again and write down any words they don't understand or take notes. Or you may want to stop the tape periodically and have students paraphrase what they have heard. Then do the exercise provided in the text. The answers are provided in the instructor's manual.

Speak Out, Skill A   The *Speak Out* activities allow students to get further practice of a skill in context. The focus is on speaking, but the exercise also involves listening to fellow students. Both whole-class and small-group activities are provided, and you may wish to vary the suggested group size. Sometimes it is advisable to put all the stronger students in one group so that they cannot dominate the weaker students. At other times it is advisable to have the stronger students dispersed among the class. It is inadvisable to allow students to form their own groups if they don't vary the groupings. Periodically changing group make-up promotes strong class rapport as well as provides a greater variety of voices and speaking styles for listening practice. The *Speak Out* activities vary in length from ten minutes to a whole class period.

Skill B   A language function is explained to the students and then is demonstrated through short conversations presented in the text and on tape. Here students learn appropriate and inappropriate use of idioms, intonation, and body language associated with the function. The conversation can be presented in several ways:

1. Students read along as they listen.
2. Students listen with books closed.
3. Students listen and repeat (when dialogues are short or you can stop the tape to allow for this).
4. Students listen and pantomime facial expressions and gestures they think the speakers would use.
5. The dialogues are also quite suitable to be modified as cloze passages with the students filling in key words as they listen.

Listen In, Skill B   This section gives the students the opportunity to listen for uses (or misuses) of the language function in the lecture and (in some chapters) in the conversations. Answers to the exercise are provided in the instructor's manual.

Speak Out, Skill B   These activities provide natural language contexts in which to practice the language function. They are designed to maximize student interaction and verbal output. The teacher should provide feedback that does not inhibit this process as the students play the various games, participate in role-plays, or team up for debates. The amount of time you spend can vary from a brief period to a whole class hour.

ACKNOWLEDGMENTS

Both people and places have contributed to the strengths of this book. First, we wish to acknowledge the people whose expertise and imagination provided not only inspiration but manuscript pages as well: Marilyn Bernstein, Steven Carlson, Steven Hollander, Steven Marx, and William G. Carter. We extend our gratitude to those who provided invaluable suggestions for the manuscript and support for our flagging spirits as we faced deadlines: Bonnie Anthony and her students; Tom and Jean Atherton; Connie Bendel; Leon Bloomfield; Lauri Carlson; Mary Dunn; Ann Feldman; Jane Gray; Chris Hepburn; Jeff Joseph; Alicia, Evie, and Sally Klein; Kim Kramer; David Marimont; Alan McCornick; John and Susan Nelson; Ed Profio; Billie Lynn, and Mickey Strauss; Ann Stromberg; Pat Sutton; Patty Werner, and Gertrude Whalley.

We also wish to thank Sandra McKay of San Francisco State University for her excellent review of the manuscript and Gail Kellersberger of the University of Houston and Susan Martel of the University of Southern Illinois for their reviews of selected chapters.

We heartily acknowledge libraries, restaurants, parks, pools and people's homes that were so graciously opened to us as havens during long hours of work and give special thanks to librarian Diane Stoll for tirelessly searching for material with a minimum of clues, to the Cal Poly Faculty Development Program, to Thomas and Judith Wasow for use of their lovely home, and to John and Mary Gill for sacrificing their privacy for the sake of the project.

Finally, we wish to express our deepest appreciation to Deana Fernández for her undaunted word processing and valuable editorial suggestions, to Eirik Børve who included us in this groundbreaking project, and to Janet Bollow Associates for their excellent work on the design and production of the text. Most of all, we are ever grateful to Mary McVey Gill for her monumental efforts in pulling such a project together, her most excellent editorial work, and her friendship.

J. F.
E. W.

MOSAIC II
A Listening/Speaking Skills Book

CHAPTER 1
LANGUAGE
AND LEARNING

In most places in the United States and Canada, children are required to go to school from age five to age sixteen. Education is required because people believe that schools help young persons develop basic skills and become useful citizens. Reading, writing, and arithmetic traditionally have been regarded as the basic skills, but most schools also teach science, history, geography, music, art, and physical education in the basic curriculum. And now in some schools, computer courses are also included. Even with such a varied curriculum, some people have questioned the value of schools for all youngsters. Do scientific geniuses or artists, for example, thrive in traditional schools, or are they stifled by them? In this chapter, you'll hear a lecture prepared for students planning to become teachers that discusses this issue.

Lecture: To School or Not to School

Skill A: Listening for the Main Point

Skill B: Requesting the Main Point

PART ONE

DISCUSSION

Most people have strong opinions about education because they have gone to school themselves. Think back to a time between the ages of five and sixteen when you were in school and share the answers to the following questions with your classmates.

1. Who was your favorite teacher? What grade were you in then? How old were you? Why was he or she your favorite? Can you recall a specific incident that explains why you liked that teacher so well?

2. Who was your least favorite teacher? Why? How old were you then? What grade were you in? Can you tell an anecdote that explains why you disliked this teacher?

3. In what ways has school been exciting? Disappointing? Do you feel you would know less, the same amount, or more if you had not gone to school? Why? If you hadn't gone to school, how would you have learned? From your parents, your parents' friends, your friends, siblings, television, radio, movies, books?

4. Do you think everyone should be required to go to school? If so, why? If not, why not? Who shouldn't be required to go to school? Should those children who don't go to school be required to fill their days with special or supervised activities? If so, what kind of activities?

VOCABULARY

Following is a list of adjectives that the speaker uses in the lecture. After the list are statements that teachers might make to describe students. Fill in the blank in each statement with the appropriate word from the list.

disciplined	*sticking to a routine, having good behavior*
gifted	*very capable and inventive*
inconsiderate	*not thoughtful about people's feelings*
moody	*frequently appearing disagreeable, unpleasant, or sad to others*
obedient	*law abiding, under control*
self-centered	*concerned primarily with oneself*

1. In nursery school, Rudy Thomas could sing his ABCs on key without missing a note. He played the piano without being taught. He made up beautiful songs by himself. By the time he was six, he must have spent six hundred hours at the piano. He probably will be a great composer or performer one day, because he's musically _gifted_.

2. Barbara Michaels sometimes seems happy, but often she seems sad or grumpy. Then she's unwilling to play with the other children. She is quite _moody_.

3. When people are talking about someone else, Toby Harrison always manages to bring the conversation around to himself. If you ask him about himself, he is very interested in the conversation and never changes the subject. Toby Harrison is very _self-centered_.

4. When Frances Paulson finishes her lunch at school, she always leaves the empty plastic wrappers and milk cartons at her place instead of throwing them away. Then the next person must clean up after her. Frances is very _inconsiderate_.

5. George Redfern, who is the kind of student that many teachers like, does whatever he is told without asking any questions. He always obeys the teacher and never gets into trouble. I, myself, find this kind of student difficult. I don't like students who are so _obedient_ and never challenge me. I find them dull and uncreative.

6. One reason Patsy Harold turns in excellent work is because she plans ahead and leaves plenty of time for each project. She never leaves her homework for the last minute. She knows how to take good notes, and she faithfully copies

them over after each class and puts them in her notebook. She is certainly a _disciplined_ student.

PART TWO

SKILL A: LISTENING FOR THE MAIN POINT

In most lectures, several main ideas are presented. These are the concepts the lecturer wants the students to remember. Often the lecturer has a general idea that serves as an "umbrella" covering the other main concepts. The student's job, then, is to pick out the main concepts, including the "umbrella" idea.

Lecturers usually begin with an _introduction_. Sometimes the main concepts and "umbrella" idea are briefly presented in the introduction; often they are not. Next comes the _body_ of the lecture. It is here that several main concepts are always presented. The final part of a lecture, the _conclusion_, is traditionally a summary of the main concepts. This is also the place where the "umbrella" idea can most easily be repeated, restated, or even introduced for the first time.

When a lecture is well organized, with a clear-cut beginning, middle, and end, the main ideas are usually easy to pick out. When a lecture is not well organized, getting the gist of what is being said is challenging, to say the least. Some lecturers are "long-winded," taking a long time to come to the point. Others ramble on and never seem to come to the point at all.

Listen In

Exercise 1   Listen to the lecture once through. Then listen again. Raise your hand when the introduction ends and the body of the lecture begins. Stop the tape and discuss how you know this. Then listen to the body of the lecture. Raise your hand when you think the conclusion begins. Stop the tape and discuss how you know this. Finish listening to the tape. In the space provided, write what you think the general or "umbrella" idea is. Compare your answer with your classmates' answers.

_____

_____

_____

_____

Exercise 2   Listen to the lecture again. This time, listen for the main ideas in the body of the lecture. Stop the tape after you hear the sentences given in the following four items. Write down the main idea of the portion of the lecture that you have just heard. When you are finished listening to the whole lecture and writing down the four main ideas, compare your answers with your classmates'.

1. Mark Twain, Charlie Chaplin, and Vincent van Gogh are examples of what we expect to find.

   _____

   _____

   _____

2. A curious child who was interested in the fresh and new, Wordsworth found his teachers sympathetic and kind.

   _____

   _____

   _____

3. Although these scientific giants experienced great conflict between the demands of school and the development of their own minds, we should not jump to conclusions.

   _____

   _____

   _____

4. He passed his medical school entrance examinations with the highest marks that any student had ever received.

   _____

   _____

   _____

Exercise 3   Do you think the lecture was well organized? Why? Poorly organized? Why? Was the lecturer long-winded, taking too much time to get to the point? Did the lecturer ramble and seem not to get to the point at all? Did you find it easy to pick out the main points? Difficult?

Speak Out

Exercise 1   Think about the variety of experiences you've had as you've acquired English or another language. Begin with the

Huck Finn and Tom Sawyer, two of Mark Twain's characters, were very mischievous and frequently stayed away from school.

Mark Twain was not a very obedient student and had very negative experiences in school.

time when you did not know one word (this may have been when you were a small child, or perhaps it was only last year) and continue up through the present time. Consider the following:

1. When were you first exposed to the language? How old were you? Have you been learning the language continuously since then, or were you interrupted for some reason?

2. Where were you? Were you in your native country or some other country?

3. Did you study this language in school? If so, where and when? What approaches or methods did your teachers use? Were any of your teachers native speakers of the language? Do you think this made a difference? Why or why not?

4. Have you had opportunities to speak this language outside the classroom with friends or family? Have you had a close boyfriend or girlfriend or perhaps a husband or wife who spoke the language?

5. Were you exposed to more than one dialect of the language? Do you think this helped or hindered your language acquisition? Why?

Break into small groups and present this information as your "English autobiography" (or other second- or foreign-language autobiography) to the members of your group. Speak for two to three minutes. As you listen to your classmates' autobiographies, note the main points.

As a class, share some of the main points of these autobiographies. Did some of you have similar language-acquisition experiences, or were they all quite different? In what ways? Were the main points dealing with personal feelings similar, or were they different? In what ways?

Exercise 2   Of course, with some speakers, it's easier to determine the main points than with others. For example, newscasters, used car salespeople, politicians, ministers, and leaders of business meetings may or may not be adept at coming to the point. And in everyday interactions with friends, family, or co-workers, there are times when we all have difficulty getting to the point.

To research this, choose three people from the following list of types of "subjects" and find an opportunity to listen to each one speak about something. Many of them can be heard on the radio or t.v. every day on their own shows or on talk shows.

artist	politician
businessperson	scientist
close friend	teacher
minister	three-year-old child
newscaster	used car salesperson

As you listen, make note of the main points and then consider these questions:

1. Which of the three speakers was the most long-winded?
2. Which one was the most succinct—that is, got to the point in the shortest time? *expressed briefly & clearly, terse*.
3. Did any of the speakers ramble so much that you felt they never got to the point? If so, which one(s)?
4. With which speaker was it easiest to get the gist of what was being said?
5. With which speaker was it hardest to get the gist of what was being said?

Share your responses to these items with your classmates and give brief descriptions of your three subjects, including approximate age and educational background. Were any correlations revealed? For example, did you and your classmates discover a correlation between profession and long-windedness? Or perhaps between age and rambling?

SKILL B: REQUESTING THE MAIN POINT

Some speakers are intentionally long-winded. For example, a United States senator who does not want a bill to be passed may filibuster, talking on and on day and night to delay the voting on the bill. Similarly, someone who is shy and timid about raising a particular issue might talk around the subject ("beat around the bush") to delay having to state the issue. Other people are unintentionally long-winded and will talk for a long time and then ask a question such as "Am I talking too much?" or "Does this make any sense?" Still others ramble on and on, never coming to the point at all. Of course, there are people who come to the point right away.

If a speaker gets directly to the point, you will not have problems understanding the gist of what is being said; however, if a speaker is long-winded or rambles, you may not be able to pick out the main points and may want to ask what they are. In these situations, if the speaker is a friend, there are many informal ways of asking what the point is. If the speaker is not a friend but an acquaintance—a supervisor or a teacher, for example—you must be careful about how you ask, so that you don't insult the person. You don't want to make the speaker feel accused of rambling or being long-winded or feel that he or she explains things poorly. With a friend, you might use the following expressions.

Requesting the Main Point (Informal)

Could you please stop beating around the bush and get to the point?
Get to the point, will (would) you please?
I don't get it. What are you talking about?
So, what are you trying to say?
So, what's the (your) point?
What are you driving at?
What are you getting at?

For more formal or sensitive situations, when you wish to be more polite, here are some expressions you might use.

Requesting the Main Point (More Formal)

One of these expressions:	*Followed by one of these:*
Excuse me.	I didn't quite catch the point.
I'm sorry.	Could you go over it again, please?
Pardon me for interrupting, but . . .	I didn't follow the last part. Could you give the main point again, please?
	I didn't understand the point you were making. Could you say it again, please? (Would you mind restating it?)
	I don't quite understand what you're getting at.

Listen to the following conversations. You will hear the expressions used appropriately and inappropriately. Sometimes the intonation is what makes the difference.

Conversation 1

In this conversation, Randy tries to tell Sandy some interesting news.

Randy: Did you see the seven o'clock news last night?
Sandy: No, what about it?
Randy: Well, they showed the wilderness-preservation march that I participated in with my ecology class. You know, the one where we went to the state capitol building and we protested and there were some people dressed up as trees and plants and stuff, and, anyway, I was really surprised at the way the newscaster handled it. Remember I told you it was raining terribly hard that day and some people were even throwing things at us and I forgot my umbrella—most people did—and we all got drenched, absolutely soaking wet. Well, the march was picked up by the major news networks and, boy, did their reports surprise me! I

didn't think the march was so controversial. It didn't feel like a very daring thing to do at the time.

Sandy: Get to the point, would you? How did the networks handle it?

This conversation was very friendly and informal, and Sandy's request for the main point was *not* impolite.

Conversation 2

Now listen to Professor Draper and a student.

Professor Draper: Well, students, I want to reorganize our schedule and change the date of the midterm. You know we had scheduled the readings by Jones and Tomfoolery for the sixteenth and the readings by Rockford and Pebble for the fourteenth and those by McVey and Gill for the twelfth. Well, I want to move McVey and Gill to the fourteenth, the midterm to the twelfth, and the Rockford and Pebble to the sixteenth and Jones and Pebble to the sixteenth and Jones and Tomfoolery to the nineteenth.
Student: So, what are you driving at? I don't get it. Are you trying to tell us that we only have two more days until the midterm?

Professor Draper did speak very quickly and the main point was not clearly stated. Still, the student's questions were impolite.

Conversation 3

Now listen to Professor Werner and a student discuss an upcoming field trip.

Professor Werner: Okay now, students, let me explain how we'll organize this plant-hunting expedition. You'll want to have a buddy and to keep your buddy with you at all times. You are to search for the various plants of the genus *Rhus*, but remember many of them are quite poisonous, so make sure your arms and legs are well covered and wear plastic gloves when you pick the plants. Of course, you will be free to wander wherever you like, but the terrain changes quickly and is unmarked. We did have a problem with students getting lost two years ago, and one of them had broken her leg.
Student: Excuse me, Professor Werner, I don't quite understand what you're getting at.
Professor Werner: Well, Richard, the point is: This trip could be dangerous if you don't follow all the rules carefully.

Professor Werner did ramble a bit, but Richard handled the situation well. He obtained the information he needed without being impolite or disrespectful.

Physicist Marie Curie loved school and was a star pupil.

Listen In

Now listen to another version of the lecture you heard. In this version, some of the main points have been omitted. During the lecture, your instructor will stop the tape so that you can ask for the main point. Each time your instructor stops the tape, several of you should practice requesting the main point by using an appropriate expression from "Skill B."

Speak Out

Look at the following incomplete conversations. Only Speaker A's first turn in the conversation is provided for you. Choose a partner and together decide who the speakers are and complete each of the conversations. Take turns being Speaker A and Speaker B. When you are Speaker B, you will probably want to use an expression for requesting the main point on your first turn. When you are Speaker A, you may answer B's request right away if you can. Otherwise, continue the dialogue with B until the gist of the conversation becomes clear to both of you.

After you practice with these conversations, try making up a few of your own, using these as models. Select the conversation that you and your partner enjoyed doing the most and present it to the rest of the class.

Conversation 1

A: Good morning, professor. Did you hear about that terrible accident on the highway last night? The traffic was backed up for hours. I hope everyone was okay. I'll bet a lot of people were late getting home, too. Probably a lot of people couldn't do some of the things they'd planned to do 'cause they got home so late. You know, almost everything closes by nine o'clock—like the public library and everything and . . .

B:

A:

B:

Etc.

Conversation 2

A: Yes—about your art project—well—oil paint is an interesting medium; the variety of textures one can achieve with oil paints is remarkable. And paper cups—yes—paper cups *do* have some interesting possibilities. And these coat hangers—it never occurred to me to use them like this. So—your sister told me you're not sure whether you're going to major in art or not. Fred

Carlson went through the same thing. Have you ever met Fred? He works over in the career counseling center now.

B:

A:

B:

Etc.

Conversation 3

A: Dad, I'd like to talk to you about something. I went over to the registrar's office yesterday. And, you know, Joan works over there. The line was really long—all the way out the door and around the building. I hadn't decided which classes to sign up for yet, but I figured that I had plenty of time to do that while I waited in line. And then I bumped into Joan and we started talking. You know, she's had the most interesting life, and she never even went to college!

B:

A:

B:

Etc.

Conversation 4

A: Do you remember that book you loaned me last week? The biography of Albert Einstein? Well, I was reading the chapter about how he developed the theory of relativity, and the phone rang. It surprised me because it was so early. No one usually calls before eight o'clock. I didn't want to get up to answer it because the chapter was so interesting. Did you know that he was only a patent clerk—he wasn't even a professor yet—when he developed that theory?

B:

A:

B:

Etc.

CHAPTER 2
DANGER AND DARING

When the need arises, it is not unusual for daring people to step forward and face danger. If a family is trapped in a burning building, a courageous neighbor might try to save the family members before the fire department arrives. And if a child, or even a dog, falls into an icy river, a passerby may not think twice about jumping right in after it. Of course, these are examples of true heroism. But what about people who face *unnecessary* dangers, dangers that have been prearranged rather than occurring by chance? What about people who jump off a bridge using only a giant elastic cord that stretches to its limit just before they hit the water, or who jump out of a plane and free-fall as long as possible before opening their parachutes? The lecture in this chapter discusses the types of people who face such dangers and what it means to be "hooked on thrills."

Lecture: Hooked on Thrills
Skill A: Noting Specific Details
Skill B: Saying "Yes" and "No"

PART ONE

DISCUSSION

In small groups, discuss the following items. Then share the highlights of your discussions with the rest of the class.

1. Do you know of any people in your native culture who seek thrills by facing unnecessary danger? If so, what type of thrill-seeking activity is most common?

2. Many thrill seekers claim that they engage in dangerous activities only for personal satisfaction; that is, that they are concerned only with increasing their self-esteem. Some critics say, however, that money is the real motive behind the most daring of these activities, and that if there were no publicity to bring fame and fortune, there would be no daredevils to perform dangerous stunts. Why do *you* think people do dangerous, daredevil stunts?

3. Which group do you think is more likely to engage in a thrill-seeking activity and why: Men or women? Young children or teenagers? Teenagers or young adults? Young children or middle-aged people?

Daredevil Stan Kruml was heading for fame and fortune as he began his run through a tunnel of fire. Halfway through he was overcome by the intense heat, and fell. He emerged from the tunnel in a ball of flame and suffered permanent damage to his hands.

Stunt Jump Thwarted

A police helicopter and emergency services officers yesterday prevented **Tony Vera,** who described himself later as a stunt man and magician, from leaping off the Manhattan tower of the Brooklyn Bridge.

Clad in a loincloth and a straitjacket, Mr. Vera, who had climbed to the top of the tower, stood on top for several minutes, having trouble fastening the straitjacket. A police helicopter hovered close to the bridge, preventing him from making a wide leap, while emergency services officers made their way up to the top.

The officers grabbed Mr. Vera and led him down to safety, and he was hustled off by the police. But before they did, Mr. Vera said: "I want some excitement in my life. I'm going to do it again. I just want to jump."

New York Times, September 13, 1980.

VOCABULARY

The following words are used in the lecture, but they are not defined by the lecturer. Read the definitions and fill in the blanks with the correct form of the word.

bizarre   *extremely odd or unusual, fanciful*

daredevil   *one who fears nothing and will attempt anything*

dominance   *power or authority*

extroversion	*interest in the world outside oneself more than in oneself*
impulsiveness	*the inclination to act suddenly, unexpectedly, or without thinking*
irresistible	*too strong to oppose or withstand*
nonconformity	*the refusal to act in accordance with generally accepted customs, beliefs, or practices*
sociopath	*a person with a personality disorder, often involving aggressive and sometimes violent anti-social behavior*
schizophrenic	*a person who has a disorder of the mind involving a complete withdrawal from reality that disturbs both emotional and intellectual functions*

/skɪzəˈfrɛnɪk/
Schizo   split personality   精神分裂症

Home work.

1. Are you willing to take great risks? Do you seek out extremely dangerous situations? If so, you are an

   daredevil.

2. Do you reject going along with the crowd? If everyone's hair is short, do you grow yours long? If so, you are an

   nonconformity

3. Have you read in the newspaper about people who kill others without any apparent reason? These people are

   sociopath.

4. Do you prefer to spend time with other people rather than

   alone? If so, you are a(n) _extroversion_

5. Do you know of anyone who loves climbing mountains? To such a person, an offer to be a member of an expedition to Nepal to climb Mount Everest would probably be

   irresistible.

6. Do you love to do things on the spur of the moment without taking much time to think them through? If so,

   you are _impulsive_.

7. Do you know someone who likes to manage all situations and be the one in charge? That person likes to show his or

   her _dominance_

8. Do you know of a man who wears makeup, dresses in Japanese kimonos and baggy pants, and wears his hair in long braids with ribbons? Some people would say this

   person is rather _bizarre_.

9. Have you ever heard about people who see things that are not really there, hear voices, or imagine that someone or something is trying to harm them? These people are

<u>schizophrenic</u>

PART TWO

SKILL A: NOTING SPECIFIC DETAILS

Once you have learned to pick out the main ideas in a lecture, your next step is to note the specific details. You will need these details later to answer questions on short-answer and multiple-choice exams. And it is also extremely important to include details when you take essay exams.

To listen for and note specific details, it is helpful to notice if the lecture is organized in the standard way, containing three sections: introduction, body, and conclusion. If so, listen for and note the main ideas in each of these sections. This will help you decide which specific details you should write in your notes. For example, if the introduction to the lecture is a recap, or summary, of what you learned in the previous class session, take notes on this material again. These notes will be an added reminder of what the lecturer thinks is important. If the introduction to the lecture is just a general introduction or an attention getter (a fact, a saying, a story, or a joke), you need not write this down unless you might like to use it later in a paper or on an exam to illustrate a point.

Next, listen for information in the body of the lecture. You will probably hear the most details in this section. Listen for names, dates, places, lists, specific examples, and other details. Write down as much information as you can in your notes, but don't worry if you can't get everything. Just put a question mark in the margin (beside the place in your notes where you are missing information) and ask a question of the lecturer or another student as soon as it is appropriate to do so.

Finally, as you listen to the conclusion, continue to make your notes as complete as possible. Most conclusions won't contain any new information, but be ready in case the instructor has forgotten to include an important detail earlier and decides to include it as an example in the conclusion.

What are some good ways to organize the main points and specific details as you write them down? One way is to use a formal outline. Look at the following examples. The one on the left is more commonly used, but many note takers find the one on the right easier to use because they don't need to remember when to use the capital and lowercase letters or roman and arabic numerals.

Outline Using Roman Numerals, Arabic Numerals, and Letters

I. Introduction
   A. Main point
   B. Main point
   C. Main point
II. Discussion/body
   C. Restatement of main point A
      1. Specific detail
      2. Specific detail
      3. Specific detail
         a. Further detail of A3
         b. Further detail of A3
   B. Restatement of main point B
      1. Specific detail
         a. Further detail of B1
         b. Further detail of B1
      2. Specific detail
   C. Restatement of main point C
      1. Specific detail
      2. Specific detail
         a. Further detail of C2
         b. Further detail of C2
      3. Specific detail
III. Conclusion
   A. Summary of IIA
   B. Summary of IIB
   C. Summary of IIC

Outline Using Only Arabic Numerals

Introduction (in paragraph form, a paraphrase of the lecturer's introductory remarks)
1. Main point
   1.1 Specific detail
   1.2 Specific detail
   1.3 Specific detail
      1.3.1 Further detail of 1.3
      1.3.2 Further detail of 1.3
2. Main point
   2.1 Specific detail
      2.1.1 Further detail of 2.1
      2.1.2 Further detail of 2.1
   2.2 Specific detail
3. Main point
   3.1 Specific detail
   3.2 Specific detail
      3.2.1 Further detail of 3.2
      3.2.2 Further detail of 3.2
   3.3 Specific detail
Conclusion (in paragraph form, a paraphrase of the lecturer's concluding remarks)

Of course, formal outlines such as these work best for note taking when the lecturer carefully organizes the material into introduction, body, and conclusion; uses one of these types of outlines as speech notes, and then sticks to the outline during the talk. But many lecturers may not do this. Some add bits of information here and there as they think of them during the lecture. Other lecturers do not use an outline format when preparing their talks. In these cases, you will need alternatives to the formal outline in order to adequately note main points and specific details. Here are five different ways to organize your notes. See which one feels the most comfortable and useful to you in your field of study.

1. This method of note taking is most useful when the main points and details are long phrases and sentences.

   Main point
   - Detail
   - Detail
   - Detail

   Main point
   - Detail
   - Detail
   - Etc.

2. This method of note taking is most useful when details are symbols, statistics, single words, or very short phrases.

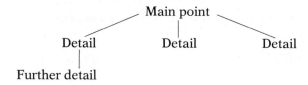

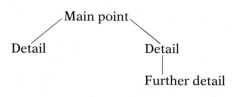

   Etc.

3. The following method is especially useful when the lecturer tends to "back up," giving specific details on points mentioned earlier in the lecture. If you leave enough space to add more details later, this type of lecture should not be problematic.

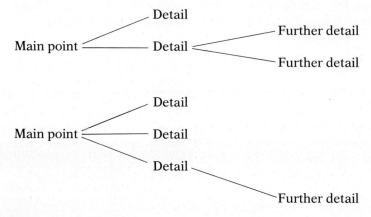

   Etc.

4. This method is useful when the lecturer states the main point after giving the details.

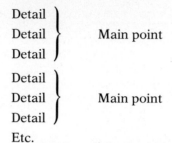

Etc.

5. This method is especially useful if the lecture is not well organized or if the lecturer does not state the main points clearly or digresses frequently. By putting all the main points on the left and details on the right, you can match them up with arrows later and double check to see if something you thought was a main point was really a detail, and vice versa.

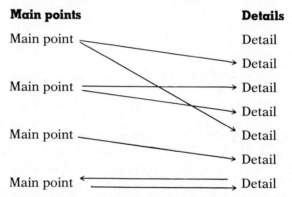

You may, of course, find it necessary to try each of these systems in turn until you become accustomed to a lecturer's style. In addition to using these basic systems of note taking, many note takers find it helpful to set things off visually by using different-colored inks or by framing certain items in boxes or circles.

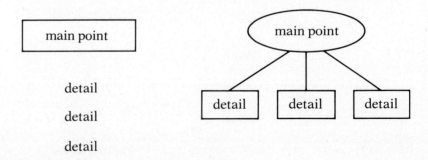

Listen In

Listen to the lecture and decide whether you should take notes on the introduction. Remember that this lecture is for a psychology class.

Your decision:

I should _____ should not _____ take notes on the introduction

because _____ .

Listen to the lecture again. This time, take notes, using one of the two lecture outline forms or one of the other five note-taking methods illustrated for you in "Skill A." Note as many specific details as you can.

Did the note-taking method you chose work well for this particular lecture? If not, choose another method and listen again as many times as necessary to get down the main points and specific details. If the method you chose did not work, you may want to listen to the lecture one or more additional times to add more detail to your notes.

Compare notes with your classmates and share your feelings about the note-taking method(s) you used.

George Willig, "the human fly," is chased by police as he climbs the World Trade Tower.

Evil Knevil broke his ankle on this leap.

Speak Out

Prepare a brief talk for your class on a daredevil stunt that you recently heard about on t.v. or the radio or read about in a magazine or newspaper. (You may need to make a trip to the library.) When you give the talk, use notes that you have made in outline form. Have your classmates take notes in outline form. After you have finished speaking, compare your outline with theirs. (You may want to put your outline on the blackboard.) Do you and your classmates have the same main points and specific details? If not, what are the differences and why do you think they occurred?

SKILL B: SAYING "YES" AND "NO"

When we are asked if we will (or would like to) do or have something, we have three basic ways to respond: *yes*, *no*, and *maybe*. *Maybe* is a neutral word meaning that at a later time your answer may be *yes* or it may be *no*. *Maybe* is exactly in the middle of the scale between *yes* and *no*, and there are no ways of saying *maybe* that are either stronger or weaker in degree. Some alternative expressions for *maybe* are *perhaps* and *possibly*.

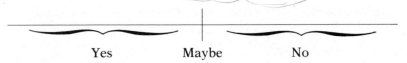

| Yes | Maybe | No |

Yes and *no*, on the other hand, can be expressed in a variety of ways. Depending on how close to or how far away from *maybe* your feelings are, you may choose either a weaker or stronger expression to say *yes* and *no*. Consider the following expressions.

Stronger Yes
   Certainly!
   Definitely!
   For sure!
   Great!
   I'll say!
   Of course!
   Okay! (strength of response indicated by intonation)
   Nothing could stop me!
   Sure!
   Sure thing!
   You bet!

Phillipe Petit balanced on a cable between two buildings 1,350 feet above the street for 45 minutes.

Weaker Yes

    I think so.
    I'm considering it.
    I'm thinking about it.
    Most likely I will (would).
    Okay. (weakness of response indicated by intonation)
    Okay, if you really want me to.
    Probably.
    That might be a good idea.

Stronger No

    Are you kidding?
    I wouldn't touch it with a ten-foot pole.
    Never!
    Never in a million years.
    No chance!
    No way!
    Not even if you (they) paid me a million dollars.
    Not for all the tea in China.
    Not me!
    Not on your life!
    Nothing doing!

Weaker No

    I don't think so.
    I doubt it.
    Not likely.
    Probably not.
    That's probably not such a good (hot) idea.

    Listen to the following conversations and notice the various ways in which the speakers say *yes* and *no*.

Conversation 1

In this conversation, Ted and Paul are discussing their plans for the weekend.

Ted: I'm going white-water rafting this weekend, Paul, and one of my buddies, Phil—you know Phil, don't you?
Paul: Uh-huh.
Ted: Well, Phil can't go because he sprained his back playing soccer, so there's room for one more. You wanna go with us?
Paul: Are you kidding? I've never gone white-water rafting.
Ted: Aw, come on. There's a minicourse being given by the Explorers' Club Tuesday and Wednesday nights this week. Take it and you'll be ready to go with us.

Paul: No way! I'll never learn enough in two nights to go on a trip for a whole weekend.

Ted: Sure you can! The instructor is great. I know of lots of people who've done it.

Paul: Well, it's probably not such a good idea, but how much does it cost?

Ted: Well, the trip'll cost you about $150 with everything—food, equipment, everything. The course is only twenty bucks.

Paul: That's not too bad. I'll think about it.

Ted: Don't just think about it; do it! You've got the money, don't you?

Paul: I think so.

Ted: Well, then, it's settled. Let's go over to the student union, have something to drink, and then sign you up.

Conversation 2

In the following conversation, Terry and Lynn are discussing vacation possibilities.

Terry: Hey Lynn, I saw the greatest trip advertised in this travel magazine I get. It's a mountain-climbing trip in Nepal—you know, in the Himalayas. We'd go all the way to the base camp on Annapurna. That means we'd follow in the footsteps of the women's expedition that climbed Annapurna in 1978! Wouldn't that be great? Let's go!

Lynn: Not on your life! You won't get me up there! I don't even like riding in those glass elevators that go up and down the outside of fancy hotels.

Terry: Come on! Think about it a bit. There's a month-long training program and then the trip is three weeks. Think how strong and brave you'll feel at the end.

Lynn: You may feel strong and brave after a month. But not me! Never in a million years!

Terry: Oh, don't be like that. It's important to overcome these fears. You'll be a better person for it!

Lynn: I won't climb a mountain! Not for all the tea in China, and that's that! Find someone else to go with you.

Terry: But I want *you* to go. You're my best friend. Besides, there won't be any technical climbing with ropes and all that—just some high-altitude hiking—really! Come on! It'll be fun. We'll have a good time!

Lynn: I like having a good time, but my idea of a good time is seeing a movie, going out to dinner, or watching a base-ball game on t.v. Wanna go out to dinner?

Terry: Definitely! Maybe I'll even convince you by the time we order dessert.

Listen In

Exercise 1   Listen to the conversations from "Skill B" again. This time, write down as many of the expressions used for saying *yes, no,* and *maybe* as you can in the spaces provided under the following five categories.

Stronger Yes

_____

_____

_____

_____

Weaker Yes

_____

_____

_____

_____

Stronger No

_____

_____

_____

_____

Weaker No

_____

_____

_____

_____

Maybe

_____

_____

_____

_____

Exercise 2   In the lecture are four examples of items from Marvin Zuckerman's "Sensation-Seeking Survey." As you hear each of these items, write down the expression that best indicates your degree of agreement or disagreement with this item.

_____

_____

_____

_____

George Willig pays his fine (1 cent per floor) to the mayor of New York City.

Speak Out

Are you very adventuresome? Do you like to take risks and try new things? Or are you more cautious and not particularly interested in new adventures? For an evaluation of your willingness to take risks, take the accompanying test and add up your score to obtain your placement on the "risk-taker ruler."

Take the test with a partner. Decide who will take the test and who will give the test first. When you are taking the test, respond to each item, using an expression from "Skill B" that best expresses your immediate reaction to the item. When you are giving the test, read each item to your partner as if you were conducting a survey and note the type of each of your partner's responses by putting a check in the appropriate column. When you have both finished taking the test, look on p. 186 for scoring instructions. When you have scored the tests, see how you measure up on the "risk-taker ruler." Share your rating with the class (if you dare!).

Risk-taker ruler.

1–30	30–60	60–100	100–130	130–160
No risk-taker You don't even like to sleep on the other side of the bed.	Low risk-taker You'll leave the house now and then.	Moderate risk-taker You might do something if your best friend does too.	Definite risk-taker You're just waiting for someone to dare you.	Hooked on thrills You can't live without risks!

RISK-TAKER TEST

Question

Would you ever . . .

Response

	Strong yes	*Weak yes*	*maybe*	*Weak no*	*Strong no*
1. try a new restaurant?	Definitely				
2. try a new popular, but rather unusual, haircut?					No way
3. try a very unusual food whose name you are familiar with (for example, chocolate-covered ants)?		Probaly			
4. try a very unusual food whose name is not familiar to you?				I doubt it	
5. explore a recently discovered island?				Never	
6. try a new laundry detergent?			Maybe		
7. try a new auto mechanic?					No chance
8. volunteer to be the first passenger in a newly designed two-seater airplane?				Are you kidding?	
9. volunteer to test a car with an experimental braking device?				Never in a million years	
10. try to climb a 15,000-foot mountain?				Not likely	
11. try to climb Mount Everest?				Not me	

27

Question	Response				
Would you ever . . .	*Strong yes*	*Weak yes*	*maybe*	*Weak no*	*Strong no*
12. parachute from a plane onto a beautiful, sweet-smelling meadow?	___	___	___	___	X
13. parachute from a plane onto the top of a skyscraper?	___	___	___	___	X
14. try skydiving stunts?	___	___	___	___	X
15. sail across the Pacific Ocean from San Francisco to Taiwan in a boat without a motor?	___	___	___	___	X
16. dive off a forty-foot cliff in Hawaii into the cool blue water below?	___	___	___	___	X
17. go out on a blind date?	___	___	X	___	___
18. go to a small party where you know only two of the seven people there?	___	___	X	___	___
19. go to a party of sixty people where you know only the host and hostess?	___	___	X	___	___
20. drive a race car at 150 miles per hour?	___	___	___	___	X
21. volunteer to take part in an experiment to test the effects of a new drug on humans?	___	___	___	___	X
22. go to a country whose language you could not read, write, or speak at all and where you did not know anyone?	___	___	X	___	___
23. cross the street against a red light?	___	___	___	___	X
24. eat a dessert for breakfast?	___	X	___	___	___
25. take part in a ritual dance while visiting a tribal village in the hills of Thailand?	___	___	X	___	___

Exercise 2 Now make up a few of your own risk-taker test questions to ask each other. Begin your questions with these or similar phrases:

Would you ever. . . ?
How would you like to. . . ?
How about. . . ?

Answer the questions, using the expressions that best describe your immediate reactions to the questions.

CHAPTER 3
MAN AND WOMAN

When young girls and boys begin to show the physical signs of becoming adult women and men, they have reached a major turning point in their development. This turning point, called puberty, can mark a transition in mental and spiritual as well as physical growth. All human beings go through puberty, but each culture has its own special puberty rites or ceremonies that acknowledge, solidify, and celebrate this monumental transition from childhood to adulthood. The lecture in this chapter describes some of the similarities and differences between the puberty rites of selected tribal cultures.

Lecture: Becoming a Man, Becoming a Woman
Skill A: Abbreviating: When and How
Skill B: Extending Congratulations and Condolences

PART ONE

DISCUSSION

Do you remember entering adolescence? What was that time like for you? In small groups, discuss the following questions.

1. Did you participate in any ceremony marking the change from childhood to adulthood (for instance, a graduation ceremony, a religious ceremony, or a social event)? If so, describe it to the class.

2. Have you ever participated in such a ceremony for someone else? If so, describe the ceremony.

3. What changes in responsibilities and relationships do you remember occurring after you reached puberty? For example, did you have greater responsibilities in your home? What were they? What about the community? Did your relationships with your friends or neighbors change? If so, how?

4. Did you change school levels at this time?

5. What new interests did you develop?

6. Were you called by any new name or nickname?

7. Did you learn to drive? Did you feel there was an association between driving and adulthood?

VOCABULARY

The definitions of the words that follow reflect the use of the words in the lecture. Study the list and choose the appropriate answer to complete the following exercise.

deprivation — *the act of taking something away; loss*

equilibrium — *the state of being in balance*

fasting — *abstaining from food*

humiliating — *lowering the pride or dignity of a person*

infected — *the condition of being diseased with a germ or virus*

isolation — *the state of being alone*

navel — *location on the body where the umbilical cord was attached to the fetus*

ordeal — *an act that tests character or endurance; a difficult experience*

suitor — *a male who courts a female*

tribal — *characteristic of a tribe or group having a common ancestor or leader*

Read the following letter from a teenager all the way through. Then go back and fill in the blanks.

Thursday, October 16

Dear Nancy,

Well, here I am at home, sick in bed. All I've got is a sore throat, but the way Mom is acting, you'd think I was *infected* with the plague or something. I don't think keeping me in *isolation*, away from everybody else, is really necessary. Nobody will catch what I have if I don't kiss them—ha! ha!

I hate just lying around. I'm getting so fat it's *humiliating* just to look in the mirror. Gosh! Ever since I turned thirteen, I just *look* at a piece of cake and I gain weight. Guess I'd better give up junk food and maybe even stop eating for a week or so. But *fasting* is such an *ordeal*. It's really tough to stop eating for a whole week. I wonder if I can make it. I don't think you can die from food *deprivation* in only a week, though!

We have a foreign exchange student from Africa living with us for a month. Her name is Desta. She's very nice, and has been telling me about customs of the various tribes in her country. In one *tribal* rite of passage, girls our age are separated from everyone for a period of time and then there is a ceremony to celebrate the girl's becoming an adult. Desta says this helps adolescents adjust to the physical and emotional changes in their lives. The puberty rites help them to maintain their *equilibrium* instead of becoming unbalanced as they go through all these changes. She has made some interesting African dishes, and she taught me some words in her language.

I've saved the best for last! Guess what! I've got a *suitor*, a real boyfriend! Herman asked me out! And he calls me every day. He's invited me to a swimming party, but Dad won't let me get the new bathing suit I want because my _*navel*_ shows when I have it on. Oh well, maybe I'll get one like it next year!

Well, got to go do my homework. Write soon!

Love,

Pam

PART TWO

SKILL A: ABBREVIATING: WHEN AND HOW

When you are taking notes in lectures, you want to record the lecturer's words as accurately as possible. The best way to do this, according to research on lecture note taking, is to use the lecturer's words as much as possible. Students who do this remember more and do better on tests than students who restate what the lecturer says in their own words as they take notes. Later, when you are writing exams or using lecture information in academic papers, you will, of course, want to put the information into your own words. Trying to write down the main points and specific details using the instructor's words can be difficult because you may write slowly and the instructor may speak quickly. But you never need to feel uncomfortable because you don't hear every word. No one hears every word, not even native speakers, and you can always ask the lecturer or a fellow student about what you have missed.

What will help you greatly, however, is knowing when and how to abbreviate as you take notes. *To abbreviate* means "to shorten," and if you are able to abbreviate sentences and words, you will be able to take down information quickly without sacrificing accuracy. There are four main ways to abbreviate. You can:

1. leave out whole words and change word order
2. omit endings, vowels, and double letters of certain words
3. use only the first, or first two or three letters of a word
4. use symbols to replace certain words or letters

To shorten sentences, you can omit articles, exclamations, unimportant prepositions, adjectives, and adverbs; use symbols; and change word order. For example, if the instructor says, "You will be expected to learn all about many ceremonies, perhaps over fifty, by the end of the term," you might write:

know over 50 ceremonies by end of term

or

learn about 50 ceremonies

Or, if the instructor says, "A greater number of males than females are born to the Yuma tribe each year," you might shorten the sentence to:

Yuma tribe : males born > females each year

or

Yuma tr : m born > f ea. yr.

If you prefer using symbols as much as possible, the previous example might look like this:

> # ♂ than ♀/yr. for Yuma

Can you guess what the instructor must have said from the following example?

Rts. of pass. impt. in all cults.

When you abbreviate, you must be careful not to use the same abbreviation for two different things. For example, if the instructor is talking about *transitions* in life and *transmission* of knowledge in the same lecture, you wouldn't want to use *trans.* for both words. Nor would you want to use *ord.* for both *ordeal* and *order.* In these cases, you need to use a different abbreviation for each term. Here's a further example. Instead of writing *boy, male,* or *man,* you can usually use the symbol ♂, and instead of writing *girl, female,* or *woman,* you can usually use the symbol ♀. But if an anthropology lecturer is discussing particular differences between what boys and men in the tribe are allowed to do, for example, it wouldn't be helpful to use ♂ for both.

Naturally, you will develop your own system of abbreviations as you go along. But experience has proven some systems to be useful time and again. For example, some students find a small raised *g* useful for shortening all *-ing* words, such as

fast g (fasting), *humiliat g* (humiliating),

or *depriv g* (depriving). Also, some students like to keep a key to their abbreviations for a particular page of notes at the top-left hand side of that page. For example:

m. = married

M. = males

unm. M. go off with tribal elders to spend time fast g.

With practice, you will find a system that makes you comfortable.

Here are three lists that should be useful when you abbreviate. The first gives some mathematical and other symbols. The second gives common abbreviations for words. Even if you don't use these words in your note taking, examining the list can help you develop your own system. The third list gives abbreviations particularly useful for taking down homework assignments.

USEFUL MATHEMATICAL AND OTHER SYMBOLS

one	1	because	$\therefore$ or $b = c$	is caused by	$\leftarrow$
two	2, etc.	before	b/4	plus, over	$+$
first	1st	equal to	$=$	minus	$-$
second	2nd	not equal to	$\neq$	money	$
third	3rd	identical to	$\equiv$	percent	%
fourth	4th, etc.	hence, therefore	$\therefore$	question	?
		intersection	$\cap$	there is	$\exists$
about, approximately	$\sim$	more than	$>$	too, to	2
and	& or +	less than	$<$		
at	@	means, causes	$\rightarrow$		

COMMONLY USED ABBREVIATIONS

a.	answer	doz.	dozen	mod.	modern
alt.	altitude, alternate	Dr.	doctor	n.b.* (from Latin *nota bene*)	note well
Amer.	American	ea.	each		
Amers.	Americans	e.g. (from Latin *ex-empli gratia*)	for example	no(s).	number(s)
atm.	atmosphere, atmospheric			pd.	paid
		ff.	following pages	pop.	population
av.	average, avenue	fr.	from	re.	regarding, concerning
b.	born	ft.	feet		
b.p.	boiling point	g.	gram	rel.	religion, returned
c. (from Latin *circa*)	about	gal.	gallon		
		id. (from Latin *idem*)	the same, identical	ret.	retired, returned
c.f. (from Latin *confer*)	compare			riv.	river
co.	company			s.	son
ct.	cents, count	i.e. (from Latin *id est*)	that is	sc.	science
cu.	cubic	jr.	junior	sr.	senior
d.	deceased, died, daughter	m.	married	stat.	statistics
				terr.	territory
dept.	department			yr.	year

*N.b. is a good abbreviation to use as a note to yourself, indicating that the lecturer has emphasized a point.

ABBREVIATIONS FOR HOMEWORK ASSIGNMENTS

ch.	chapter	**p.**	page
ev. #'s	even numbers	**pp.**	pages
l	learn	**q.**	question(s)
od. #'s	odd numbers	**st.**	study

A teenager from Taos Pueblo, New Mexico.

Listen In

Exercise 1   Listen to the lecture and take notes as you would for a regular classroom lecture. Use as many abbreviations as you can. You may find some of the abbreviations introduced in this chapter useful. You may also want to create some of your own.

Exercise 2   Compare your notes with a classmate's. If you see any abbreviations your classmates used that you think would be useful, use them yourself as you listen to the lecture a second time. Then share your abbreviations with the class. Put the abbreviations on the blackboard, perhaps in alphabetical order. Leave them on the blackboard and take notes again.

Speak Out

Exercise 1   We encounter abbreviations and symbols in a variety of situations every day. As a class, decide what these abbreviations stand for.

1. ASAP (on a business memo)
2. FYI (on a business memo)
3. RGH RIDR (on an auto license)
4. ANML DOC (on an auto license)
5.

6. SOS
7. Marge cd. @ 7:00, call bk.
8. H_2O
9. thanx
10. Merry Xmas
11. rt. on

Exercise 2   Look for examples of symbols and abbreviations in your daily life. (You'll probably need to spend a couple of days looking.) Bring them to class, put them on the blackboard, and

let your classmates guess where you found them and what they mean.

Exercise 3 In groups of three, make up abbreviations for auto license plates. Use only the number of letters allowed in your state or area. Put the abbreviations on the board and have your classmates guess their meanings. Then create two messages using abbreviations that you could use on a T-shirt. Put these on the board and have your classmates guess what these T-shirt messages are.

SKILL B: EXTENDING CONGRATULATIONS AND CONDOLENCES

On the occasions that mark transitions in the lives of people you know, you are usually expected to say something appropriate. Whether or not friends and family prepare formal rites, ceremonies, or celebrations marking these transitions, people use certain expressions (which have become rituals in themselves) to convey feelings on these occasions.

Many rites of passage are happy occasions, occasions when you wish to offer congratulations: the birth of a child, graduation from one level of school to the next, a marriage, and even retirement. In contrast, you offer condolences for a loss. This might be a death: the death of an aged parent or grandparent, a friend or spouse, or a child. Or you may, for example, find yourself in the unfortunate position of needing to offer condolences for the loss of a job.

When you wish to extend congratulations, you can say "Congratulations" and follow this up with a phrase expressing your good wishes appropriate to the particular occasion. Here are some of the expressions most often used for this purpose.

Extending Congratulations

Congratulations! (plus one of the following)

For something new, for example, a new baby, job, car; an award; a raise; an engagement:

I'm so happy for you!
I'm so pleased for you!
I'm thrilled for you!
I'm tickled for you!
That's (It's) wonderful (terrific, great)!
That's great news!
It couldn't have happened to a nicer person!

For birthdays:

May you have many more.
May you have a hundred more.
Many happy returns (of the day).
I wish you all that you wish for yourself.

For weddings:

(I wish you) All the best in the years to come.
All the (my) best to you (both).
May you have a long and prosperous life together.

For graduation:

I'm sure you'll have much success in the years to come.
I know you've got a great future ahead of you.

Extending condolences is, of course, more difficult than extending congratulations and best wishes. On occasions of loss and grief, you want to choose the most appropriate and sensitive words with which to express your feelings and offer comfort. Here are some expressions most commonly used for this purpose.

Extending Condolences

One of these expressions:

I'm so (terribly, extremely) sorry.
I can't tell you how sorry I am.
My thoughts are with you (and your family).
My condolences to you (and your family).
All my sympathy to you in this trying time.

Followed by one of these (optional):

Is there anything I can do?
Let me know if there's anything you need.
Can I help out in any way?
If there's anything I can do to help, please don't hesitate to ask.

If you don't feel comfortable with any of these expressions and you just don't know what else to say, but feel you must say something, just be honest and put it this way:

I'm sorry. I just don't know what to say.
I can't express how sorry I am.

Both of these expressions are polite and sensitive, and most people will understand exactly what you mean, the intention of your words.

When you extend congratulations or condolences, not only is it important to use the right words, you must be aware of tone of voice as well. For example, if your tone of voice expresses indifference, no number of enthusiastic words of contragulations will convince listeners that you are truly happy for them.

Listen to the following pairs of brief conversations, which express congratulations. In the first of each pair, the congratulations sound sincere; contrast the first with the second of each pair of exchanges.

A: Guess what! I'm getting married next month!
B: Oh! Terrific! I'm so happy for you.

A: Guess what! Louise and I are engaged!
B: Congratulations. I'm so happy for you.

A: Hey! I've got some news! I got a promotion at work.
B: Congratulations! I'm so pleased for you.

A: Hey, listen to this! I got a raise this week.
B: No kidding! Congratulations! I'm thrilled.

A: It's my ninetieth birthday today!
B: Congratulations! May you have many more!

A: Guess what! I'm twenty-five years old today!
B: Congratulations! Many happy returns!

Now listen to the following exchange, in which congratulations are extended as part of an ongoing conversation.

A: Boy! The traffic downtown sure was terrible today.
B: Yeah—sure was. Are you still having trouble with your car overheating in heavy traffic?
A: Oh, no! I finally got a new car.
B: Congratulations! What kind of car did you get?
A: A blue Toyota with all the extras.
B: Great! Does it get good mileage?
A: Sure does! It's so much better than my old car!
B: Well I'm really glad to hear that! Use it in the best of health!
A: Thanks! I will!

And now listen to this conversation, in which condolences are extended.

A: What have you been up to lately?

B: Not much—just work, work, and then a little more work. But things will look brighter when we get this project finished in December.

A: Are you still driving to Los Angeles every week to take care of your mother?

B: No, I'm not doing that anymore. She died in September.

A: Oh! I'm so sorry. Is there anything I can do?

B: No, I don't think so. Everything's under control now. My father had a rough time for a while, but he's doing much better now.

A: I just can't tell you how sorry I am.

B: Oh, no, you mustn't be! It was for the best. She was suffering so much.

A: Yes, I suppose so. Well, please give my condolences to the rest of your family.

B: Yes, I will. Thanks so much.

Listen In

During the first portion of the lecture, the instructor mentions a variety of occasions for which either congratulations or condolences might be in order. And during the rest of the lecture, the instructor mentions a few more. Listen to the lecture and note as

many occasions as you can that might require either congratulations or condolences. Compare your notes with your classmates'. Then, as a class, choose expressions from "Skill B" that would be appropriate for each of the situations in your notes.

Speak Out

Exercise 1   For the following occasions, think of the expressions of congratulations or condolences that you would say in your native language. Then translate these expressions into English and share them with your classmates. How similar are these expressions to each other and to the English ones listed in "Skill B"?

1. An engagement   *congratulations! I could'nt wait to attend your wedding.*
2. At a wedding: to the bride's or groom's parents and to the newly married couple   *May you have a good son as soon as possible!*
3. A pregnancy   *I wish that's a boy.*
4. Birth of a baby   *How pretty he/she is!*
5. Graduation from kindergarten
6. Job promotion
7. New purchase   *What a good bargain! (deal)*
8. Retirement   *Enjoy your life*
9. Job loss   *There are other good chances waiting for you.*

43

10. Death of a friend *I'm sorry! Please keep your sadne...*
11. Death of a relative
12. Serious accident of a friend or relative *May you well as soon as possible*

Exercise 2   Choose a partner and together work out dialogues for a few of the following congratulations and condolences. In each situation, you must decide what might be said before and what might be said after the congratulations and condolences. Change partners if you wish and work out a few more. Present your favorite to the class.

1. Congratulations! I'm so happy for you. When do you expect the new arrival?
2. I'm so sorry. How did it happen?
3. I'm so sorry. How sad you must feel. Is there anything I can do?
4. Congratulations! Who's the lucky person?
5. Congratulations! And what are your future plans?
6. Congratulations! What's his/her name?
7. I can't tell you how sorry I am. How's your mother doing?
8. Congratulations! I'm so pleased for you! When do you start?
9. Congratulations! That's great news! What time?
10. I'm sorry. I just don't know what to say. Please call me if you need anything.
11. Oh, that's terrible. I'm so sorry. Do you have any other possibilities?

CHAPTER 4
MYSTERIES PAST AND PRESENT

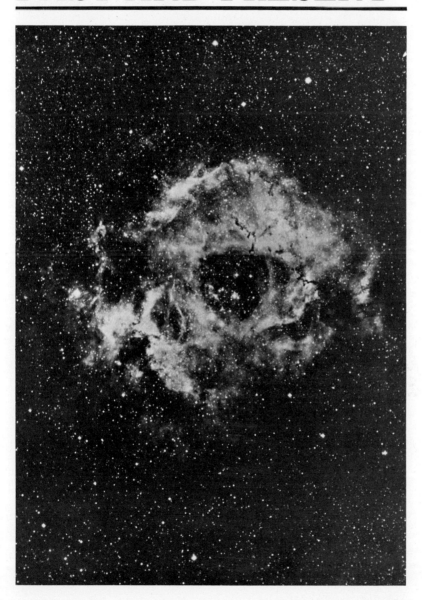

The urge to solve a mystery, to figure out the puzzle and find the answer is a basic part of human nature. When you look at the solar system and consider how it was formed, you are faced with one of the most profound mysteries of the universe. The lecture in this chapter is about the origin of our solar system and how various philosophers and scientists worked as sleuths (detectives) to try to solve this mystery.

Lecture: The Origins of Our Solar System

Skill A: Using Illustrations in Note Taking

Skill B: Admitting Lack of Knowledge
about Something

PART ONE

DISCUSSION

As a class or in small groups discuss the following:

1. Which planets in the solar system can you name? Which planet is closest to the sun? Which one is farthest away? Which one is closest to the earth? In small groups, label the diagram as

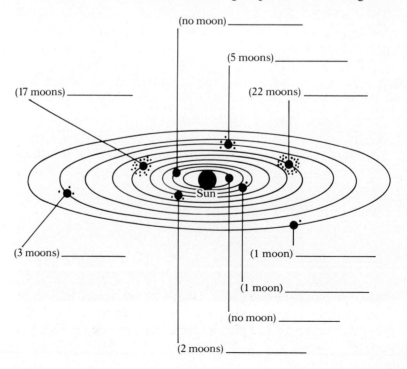

(no moon) _____

(5 moons) _____

(17 moons) _____   (22 moons) _____

(3 moons) _____   (1 moon) _____

(1 moon) _____

(no moon) _____

(2 moons) _____

well as you can. If you know the names of the planets in English, write in English. If you don't, write them in your native language. (*Hint:* the number of moons or natural satellites is written as a numeral next to each planet.) As a class, compare the names of each of the planets. What languages are represented among the class members? What similarities among the various languages do you notice for the names of each planet?

2. What stories, myths, or folktales do you know about the origin of the solar system? Share these with your classmates. What similarities in the stories did you notice among the different cultures in the class?

3. What scientific theories about the origin of the solar system have you been taught in school? Share these theories with your classmates.

VOCABULARY

contraction	elements	mass
dense	hypothesis	to speculate
electromagnetic field	lump	sphere

Idioms:

to bear in mind
bottom line
to get right down to it

The following sentences contain words and idioms the lecturer uses in a context that defines the word or idiom. Read the item and fill in your own definitions. Compare your answers with your classmates'.

1. Most scientists say that the universe is in a state of expansion— that it is getting larger; however, there are a few scientists who argue that some regions of the universe are not in a state of expansion, but rather a state of *contraction.*

   Contraction means _____

   _____

   _____

2. A magnet is a piece of metal that can attract iron. When a piece of metal is made into a magnet by the use of an electric current, the magnet is called an electromagnet. Interestingly, in outer space we find places where there are *electromagnetic fields.*

An *electromagnetic field* is _____

_____

_____

3. To demonstrate to the class the relative sizes of the planets, the instructor took balls of different sizes and placed them at various distances from a very large globe, which represented the sun. These *spheres* were of many different colors, and the students were immediately interested in what the colors indicated about the planets.

Sphere means _____

_____

_____

4. When we study objects in space, we are often concerned with the size or volume of the object and what it is made of. We want to know, for example, if the *mass* is a solid or a liquid.

Mass means _____

_____

_____

5. Astronomers who work on developing theories of the origin of the planets seem to enjoy their work, which mainly involves sitting and thinking. They take certain ideas and theorize about what the results would be *if* these ideas were true. These results or conclusions then need to be tested to see if the ideas are indeed true. Unfortunately, it is often difficult for the astronomers to get enough money to test their *hypotheses*. They may struggle for years before they are given the money that gives them a chance to do so.

Hypothesis means _____

_____

_____

6. "Take these small pieces of clay," the instructor told the students, "and put the *lumps* together to build your own model of the solar system. Of course, you don't have to use clay. You could use lumps of dough or papier mâché if you prefer."

Lump means _____

_____

_____

7. Another question astronomers ask about objects in space is this: How *dense* is the object? They need to know how close the molecules in the object are to each other. Often they use special photography to find the answer.

Dense means _____

_____

_____

8. Scientists *speculate* about what *elements* might be found in the objects in space. Based on what they know about the frequency of different elements in the universe, they can say that a certain proportion of iron, hydrogen, or mercury, for example, is likely to be found in these objects.

To speculate means _____

_____

_____

Element means _____

_____

_____

9. *"Bear in mind,"* said the professor as a reminder to the students, "that we'll have an astronomy quiz each Thursday from now to the end of the term."

To bear in mind means _____

_____

_____

10. "You must have a passing average to complete this course," he went on. "The *bottom line* is that no one with less than a 70 average passes." (See item 11 for an additional example of the use of *bottom line.*)

Bottom line means _____

_____

_____

11. "You know," said the astronomy professor, "you'll learn a lot about astronomy in this course. Astronomers have learned an enormous amount in the last hundred years. But when you *get right down to it,* what we've learned is that what we don't know is far greater than what we do know. The *bottom line* is that our ignorance surpasses our knowledge."

To get right down to it means _____

_____

_____

PART TWO

SKILL A: USING ILLUSTRATIONS IN NOTE TAKING

A major problem for many students is remembering accurately the important information given in a lecture. The best solution to this problem is to take notes, using the lecturer's own words as much as possible. But you don't need to write every word the lecturer says. For example, you can abbreviate what the lecturer says. (See Chapter 3, "Skill A.") And you can also use diagrams and pictures to illustrate what the lecturer says. There is a saying, "One picture is worth a thousand words"; one quickly and accurately drawn diagram can save you many sentences of writing.

When are the best times to take down a lecturer's words as pictures? You can do this most easily when the lecturer is speaking about the relationships between two or more objects or ideas. For example, if the instructor says, "Consider two stars, the second one being about twice as big as the first, and think of the smaller one as rapidly approaching the larger one," you might draw:

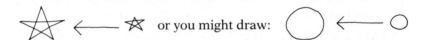

Later, the lecturer may name the stars and ask you to label them. Then you need only go back to your original drawing and add the labels. For instance, if the lecturer says, "Now, for the sake of convenience, let's call the larger star LS and the smaller star SS," your drawing would look like this:

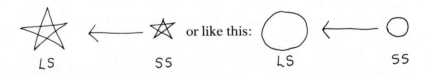

Of course, when you are drawing, you need to be careful. If your drawing could represent only the objects the instructor is describing, as in the first drawing, you need not label the objects. However, if the drawing could represent many objects, you must label them so you will be certain to understand your notes when you want to use them later for review. The circles in the second drawing, for example, could be stars, planets, satellites, novas, or snowballs. When you reread your notes, you want to feel secure that you can tell the planets from the stars. Or, to take another example, if the lecturer says, "According to Tycho Brahe, planets travel in concentric circles around the sun, but then travel as a unit around the Earth," you might draw and label a diagram like the following one. Later, when you look back at your lecture notes, this type of diagram should be clear.

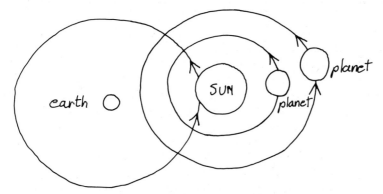

Of course, any pictures or diagrams your instructor puts on the board should be copied into your notes. For example, if your instructor puts on the board a diagram of concentric circles like the following one representing the planet orbits, you will want to copy the drawing into your notes.

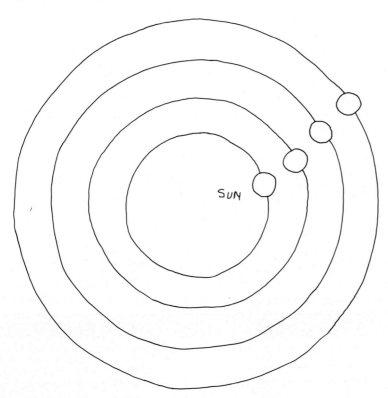

Listen In

Listen to the lecture once through to become familiar with the scientific concepts introduced. Then look at the following list of hypotheses, some of which have been illustrated for you as examples. Then listen to the lecture and supply the missing illustrations.

1. Descartes's vortices theory

   a. Hot cloud of dust and gases

   b. Cooling cloud becomes central body with smaller bodies revolving around it

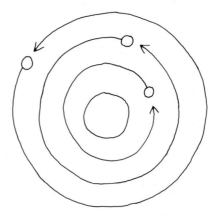

2. Kant and Laplace's nebular hypothesis

3. Jeans and Jeffries's gravitational attraction hypothesis

4. Alfvén's plasma-nebular hypothesis
   a. Rotating protostar sets off thermonuclear reaction

   b. At first, disk rotates more slowly than center sphere

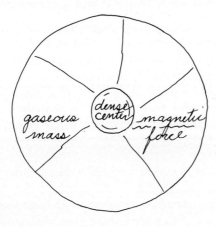

c. Later, disk rotates faster than center sphere and cooling causes lumps to form, which eventually become planets and moons

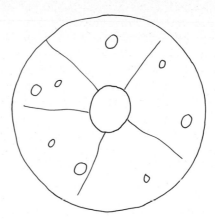

Speak Out

Exercise 1   Choose a partner for this activity. You are travelers in space approaching an uncharted solar system. Describe what you see through the window of your space capsule as you approach the solar system. Your partner takes notes on what you say, using illustrations. You might say, "The third planet to the left of the sun is twice the size of the planet closest to the sun," for example. Be sure to include the following in your description:

- the size of the sun in relation to the planets
- the number and size of planets in relation to each other
- the distance of each planet from the sun
- the number of moons each planet has (if any)
- any unusual characteristics of any of the planets (for example, any planet that always faces the sun so that half the planet is in darkness)
- any other objects, such as spaceships and meteors

When you have finished your description, look at your partner's drawing and discuss how well you think it fits with what you tried to describe. Name the planets if you like. Then it will be your partner's turn to describe an uncharted solar system for you to draw. To make this activity more interesting, put a barrier of some sort between you and your partner so that the speaker cannot correct the notetaker/illustrator as you go along. Or simply sit back-to-back.

Exercise 2   Imagine you're a space explorer and you've chosen to explore one of the planets in the uncharted solar system you described. You are expected to report to Mission Control what you see of both sides of the planet from your ship, and then Mission

Control will tell you exactly where to land. As the space explorer, you might see some rather extraordinary sights. For example, "On one side of the planet I see three large bodies of water, and the funny thing is that they are all shaped like letters of the alphabet. The first, at the upper left, is shaped like an E. The second, right below it, is shaped like an R, and the third, in the upper right, is shaped like a G. The land masses seem to have metallic mountains running horizontally across them. Between the mountains are meadows of crystal. There are seven cities . . ." and so on. Choose a partner. Decide which one of you will be the space explorer first and which will be the contact person at Mission Control. Again, you might wish to put a barrier between you and your partner or sit back-to-back. When the person taking notes has a "good picture" of the planet, change roles and do the activity again.

When you've finished, perhaps a few students can volunteer to give their descriptions of the planet to the entire class. As the descriptions are given, class members can take turns drawing the various parts of the planet on the board.

SKILL B: ADMITTING LACK OF KNOWLEDGE ABOUT SOMETHING

In countries such as the United States and Canada, a person's ability to admit lack of knowledge about something is valued. Students will often criticize an instructor who is unwilling to admit ignorance and will compliment an instructor who *is* willing to admit ignorance. And the same holds true for fellow students. How do we admit our ignorance? There are many ways to do this, but some are better than others in certain situations. Here are some formal and informal ways to admit lack of knowledge.

Formal

I'm afraid . . . I'm sorry, but . . .	I don't know. I couldn't (can't) tell you. I'm not sure. I don't remember. I can't remember. I forget. It's slipped my mind.

If you add a reason for your lack of knowledge, your words will sound even more polite:

Example: Do you know where the post office is?

No, I'm afraid I can't. I'm from out of town myself.

Informal

The following expressions can be rude, depending on the information or the situation, but they are used frequently among friends.

Beats me.

(I) Can't (couldn't) even begin to guess (say).

Don't ask me.

(I) Haven't (got) a clue.

(I) Haven't the foggiest (idea).

How do I know?

I give up!

I have no idea.

I'm sure I don't know.

It's beyond me.

Now listen to the following conversations.

1. **Tourist 1:** Excuse me, sir, could you give me directions to the Statue of Liberty?

   Tourist 2: I'm sorry, I don't know. I'm not from around here myself.

2. **Samantha:** Professor Hill, what did the Druids believe about the origin of the universe?

   Professor Hill: I'm afraid I don't remember the answer to that anymore, Samantha, but almost any text on Druid history should tell you.

3. **Phil:** When is the next space shuttle supposed to take off?

   Bob: Beats me. I haven't a clue.

4. **Carmine:** How long does it take to climb Machu Picchu?

   Dorothy: Don't ask me. I haven't any idea.

5. **Gary:** When were the statues on Easter Island carved?

   Sarah: I'm sure I don't know!

Listen In

Exercise 1 Listen to the lecture and write the expressions the lecturer and students use to express lack of knowledge.

_____

_____

_____

_____

_____

_____

A view of Venus from the Pioneer Orbiter.

_____

_____

_____

_____

Exercise 2   Listen to the conversations again. In which cases is the second speaker polite? Rude? Discuss the alternatives with your classmates.

Speak Out

Exercise 1   Think of any unexplained phenomenon or mystery that you know about and compile ten questions about it. Try to have five questions that people will probably be able to answer and five questions that they will probably not be able to answer.

Example: Where is Stonehenge? (Some students will probably be able to answer.)

How did the Druids move the rocks at Stonehenge? (No one knows for certain.)

Choose a partner and take turns asking and answering the questions. Answer the questions if you can, but when you don't know the answer, don't hesitate to admit your lack of knowledge by using an expression from "Skill B." Use a variety of expressions.

When you finish, change partners and do the activity again. Then change partners several more times if time permits. You may want to eliminate some of your questions and add a few others for variety as you go along.

Exercise 2   Now think about some less mysterious phenomena such as "Where's the cap for the toothpaste?" "Why can't I find my car keys when I'm late for class?" "What are the blue reflectors in the streets for?" or "Why does Roger eat his salad after he eats the main course rather than before?" Jot down at least ten questions of this kind and ask them to each other in the same manner as you did in Exercise 1. Again, practice using the expressions for admitting lack of knowledge. You can also use this activity to give yourself the opportunity to try various tones of voice, from polite to indifferent to irritated to downright rude.

CHAPTER 5
TRANSITIONS

In some ways life is like a puzzle. To construct a puzzle, you gather and put together parts. Similarly, people gather and put together life's experiences. They take these experiences as life's lessons and assimilate them. By piecing together what they have learned, they grow into mature adults.

However, unlike a puzzle that is complete at a definite point in time, human beings never stop growing. People continue learning and going through transitions at each stage of life. In the lecture in this chapter, you will hear about what the character Jacques in Shakespeare's play *As You Like It* had to say on the subject of life's changes.

Lecture: Jacques' View of the Stages of Life

Skill A: Understanding and Making Analogies

Skill B: Making Negative Statements
               or Comments Politely

PART ONE

DISCUSSION

As a class or in small groups, discuss the following:

1. Everyone has experienced at least a few major transitions in life. These might include changing schools, losing someone close, or just getting another year older and facing the responsibilities and privileges that come at a particular age. Share at least two such transitions that you've faced and what they meant to you. When you were going through these transitions, did you feel "in control" or did you feel caught by the circumstances and events surrounding these times?

2. Do you think people have much influence over their own growth and development (physical, mental, and emotional)? Or do you think that "free will" does not play much of a part in the course of life and that human beings are like puppets whose strings are pulled by forces beyond their control? Why?

3. Assume for the moment that you do indeed direct your own life or "pull your own strings," as the expression goes. What

do you personally want to achieve to feel successful? (Give at least one example.) What are the steps you plan to take to make this happen?

4. Consider the following analogies about time. What do you think they mean? Does any one of them hold any particular significance for you? Why? If you can, tell about an event or time in your life when one of these quotations might have been significant. Let your classmates guess which quotation best applies to the situation you describe.

> Time wasted is existence, used [it] is life.
> —Henry Wadsworth Longfellow

> I recommend you take care of the minutes, for the hours will take care of themselves.
> —Lord Chesterfield

> Unhappy is he who trusts only to time for his happiness.
> —Voltaire

VOCABULARY

Exercise 1   Find a word on the right that defines each italicized word on the left.

enlarged

anger

1. __b__ An *inflated* self-image is something like a balloon *inflated* with hot air.

a. compelled to do something
b. blown up, enlarged
c. anger, rage
d. to frighten
e. dishonest
f. intense emotion

2. __c__ People who believe that we are like puppets and have little control over our lives may feel that our efforts in life will produce only "sound and *fury*" and in the end will not mean anything.

dishonest

3. __e__ Many politicians have been found to be extremely *corrupt* individuals who are interested only in money and power, not in the public welfare.

intense emotion

4. ____ Some people believe that *passion* is the cause of much suffering in life, while others believe that *passion* is the only thing that makes life worth living.

to frighten

5. ____ Extremely confident and strong-willed people can easily *intimidate* others who are shy and less confident.

intimidate
intimate (very closely connected)

compelled to do something

6. ____ The man was so *driven* by ambition that he rarely went home from work until ten or eleven at night.

Exercise 2   Discuss the following questions.

1. Did you ever feel as if you were *in a rut* and wanted to make a major change in your life? If so, when? Why?

not interesting.

to be in a rut   *things are boring.*   *dull*

2. Do you think it's important *to make a name for yourself* in life? Why or why not?

3. What are some of the things you would do *at the drop of a hat*? (For example: Help a friend in trouble? Eat a piece of chocolate cake? Go for a swim in the ocean?)

spontaneously
impulsively

4. There's a fine line between honesty and rudeness. But sometimes you have to speak out and say something in a straightforward manner, in other words *put it bluntly*. When was the last time you had to do this? What were the circumstances? What did you say?

frankly
real

5. Sometimes it seems that certain laws of irony operate in the universe. For example, Jeremy called Susan to invite her to a party and left a message about the party with her roommate. When Susan called back two hours later, Jeremy rushed to answer the phone and fell and broke his arm. It was bad enough that he had broken his arm, but *to add insult to injury*, it turned out that Susan was planning to go to the party with someone else instead. What have been some of the ironies in your life, or cases in which insult was added to injury?

two bad thing
add at all

PART TWO

SKILL A: UNDERSTANDING AND MAKING ANALOGIES

This chapter began with the expression, "Life is like a puzzle." This expression is an example of figurative language—that is, language used to create an image and not meant to be taken literally. An analogy is an example of figurative language. It is a comparison, showing the logical relationship between two things. Here are some examples:

An idea is like a seed.

History is merely gossip.
—Oscar Wilde

Love is food for the soul, but jealousy is poison.

Life is a disease. The only difference between one man and another is the stage of the disease.
—George Bernard Shaw

If you can paraphrase a statement as an equation, it is an analogy. For example, the four analogies given as examples can be represented by the following equations.

idea = seed   love = food for the soul
history = gossip   life = disease

Analogies make language more interesting and vivid and are powerful conveyors of meaning. They do not have to be complex; in fact, they can be quite simple. It is common for people to use analogies to help others understand what they are trying to say. Therefore, it is important for you to be able to recognize analogies and to know the difference between literal and figurative language as you develop your listening skills. The following expressions are often used in making analogies:

about the size (shape, color, etc.) of   is (are) almost (just) like
as   mean(s)
as . . . as   seem(s) like
is (are) the same as   is (are) similar to

Listen In

Jacques from Shakespeare's *As You Like It.*

English 107
Introduction to Shakespeare

JACQUES' SPEECH FROM <u>AS YOU LIKE IT</u>

All the world's a stage,
And all the men and women merely players.
They have their exits and their entrances,
And one man in his time plays many parts.
His acts being seven ages. At first the infant,
Mewling and puking in the nurse's arms,
Then the whining schoolboy, with his satchel
And shining morning face, creeping like a snail
Unwillingly to school. And then the lover,
Sighing like a furnace, with a woeful ballad
Made to his mistress' eyebrow. Then a soldier,
Full of strange oaths, and bearded like a pard,
Jealous in honor, sudden and quick in quarrel,
Seeking the bubble reputation
Even in the cannon's mouth. And then the justice,
In fair round belly with good capon lined,

With eyes severe, and beard of formal cut,
Full of wise saws and modern instances,
And so he plays his part. The sixth age shifts
Into the lean and slippered Pantaloon,
With spectacles on nose and pouch on side,
His youthful hose, well saved, a world too wide
For his shrunk shank, and his big manly voice,
Turning again toward childish treble, pipes
And whistles in his sound. Last scene of all,
That ends this strange eventful history,
Is second childishness and mere oblivion,
Sans teeth, sans eyes, sans taste, sans
everything.

Exercise 1   Listen to the lecture all the way through for the main ideas. Then listen again for the analogies the speaker uses. Make a tally each time you hear an analogy (卌 . . .). How many did you pick out? Do you remember any in particular? If so, which ones? Share your answers with your classmates.

Exercise 2   Look over the following items. Then listen to the lecture for the third time. As you listen, complete the analogies. Use the lecturer's words if there's time, or use your own words, perhaps in the form of an equation.

Examples: A Buddhist would probably see transformation or change as _an opportunity for spiritual growth._

A business executive may see change as _financial loss or gain._

1. Planning, working, and struggling for success are like _____

2. One disturbing vision is the idea that we are just _____

3. Or even worse than this idea is the notion that we are just ___

4. The seven stages of life are _____

5. The schoolboy creeps to school like _____

_____

6. A young person in love may be accused of sighing like _____

_____

7. When the lecturer says the hero burns with desire, he means that desire is like _____

_____

8. The young hero thinks that becoming a man is _____

_____

9. The young soldier grows a beard so he will look as fierce ____

_____

10. As the man grows older, he loses the clear voice of youth. Now his voice _____

_____

11. Reaching old age, the man has almost come full circle. He is now like _____ again.

12. And death is _____

_____

Speak Out

Exercise 1   In small groups, think of as many analogies as you can for each of the following items. One way to do this is to "free associate"—that is, to see what pops into your head when you hear each item. Then make an analogy comparing the item with the association that just came to you. Or, you may prefer to be more deliberate and analytical in devising your analogies.

Example: time

        time = change

        Time is like a river, constantly changing yet always the same.

        Time is a double-edged sword that cuts in two ways, bringing both the joy and sorrow of change.

1. love
2. infatuation
3. passion
4. sorrow
5. life
6. death
7. youth
8. old age
9. a cynic

10. a realist	**12.** a woman	**14.** imperfection
11. a man	**13.** perfection	**15.** ambition

Exercise 2   Share some of your group's analogies with the rest of the class by playing the following guessing game. Consider all the analogies your group created and, as a group, select a few favorites. Now substitute the pronoun *it* for the subject of each of these analogies and see if the rest of the class can guess which item you are talking about.

Example: *It* is like a river, constantly changing yet always the same.

   Time.

SKILL B: MAKING NEGATIVE STATEMENTS OR COMMENTS POLITELY

Many times there is only a fine line between honesty and rudeness. This is especially true when what is being said is negative or critical. The negative comment may be based on accepted fact, or it may be just a personal opinion, in which case the thin line between honesty and rudeness becomes even thinner. Therefore, when you find yourself in a situation in which you feel compelled to make a negative statement, you can use one of the following expressions, said in a sympathetic, sincere tone of voice.

Actually . . .
Frankly . . .
Honestly . . .
I'm sorry to tell you . . .
Let's face it . . .
Not to beat around the bush . . .
To be frank . . .
To be honest with you . . .
To put it bluntly . . .
To tell the truth . . .

If the expression and the negative statement following it are not delivered in a sympathetic, sincere tone, they will not have the desired effect. For example, if your voice sounds sarcastic, angry, or impatient, your words will convey only these feelings and you will sound rude. Listen to the following conversations.

Conversation 1

Mickey: Gloria, have you seen my cousin Ted lately?
Gloria: Yeah, I saw him last week at the club meeting.
Mickey: Oh really? How was he?

Gloria: Well, to be honest with you, I don't think he looked very good. He seemed so thin and pale and . . . well, just old.

Mickey: Well, he's been working very hard and, let's face it, he's no youngster anymore. I've been trying to persuade him to retire, but he just won't do it.

The previous conversation conveyed concern and sympathy. Now listen to the same conversation delivered in an entirely different tone of voice. It's a good thing Ted doesn't overhear this one!

Conversation 2

Now listen to this conversation between a father and daughter.

Miranda: Dad, I've something to tell you.
Mark: What is it, sweetheart?
Miranda: Jeremy asked me to marry him.
Mark: And?
Miranda: And I said yes. We'd like to be married right away. What date this month would be best for you?
Mark: To put it bluntly, no date! I'm sorry to tell you, but if you decide to go ahead with this plan, I won't be at the wedding.

In the previous conversation, Mark was indeed sorry that he wouldn't be at the wedding. Perhaps he will be away on business in the next few weeks. Now listen to the same conversation delivered in another tone. This time, Mark clearly has a different sort of reason for not coming to the wedding.

Conversation 3

In this conversation, Paul asks Jane for her honest opinion.

Paul: Well, how do you like it? I know it's not professional quality yet. I've only taken one course. But what do you think? Should I quit my job and become a photographer instead?
Jane: To tell the truth, I can't make out what that is.
Paul: It's a bird soaring over a rainbow. See the little point here? That's the beak. Well, what do you think?
Jane: Well, not to beat around the bush . . . don't quit your job just yet.

In the previous conversation, Jane was trying to be as kind as possible. Now listen to the same conversation, but this time Jane doesn't care if she hurts Paul's feelings.

Listen In

Exercise 1 In the lecture, the instructor uses various expressions to make negative statements or comments. Listen to the lecture and jot down as many of these expressions as you can in the spaces

All the world's a stage . . .

provided beside the numbers in the following exercise. The first one has been done for you. What can you tell about the lecturer's attitude from her tone of voice? Share your responses with your classmates.

Exercise 2 Listen to the lecture again. This time, write the negative statements that follow each of the expressions. You may either write the statements word for word or paraphrase them. The first one has been done for you. Share your responses with your classmates.

1. *Let's face it.*
   Time and change inevitably bring decline and death.

2. _____

   _____

   _____

3. _____

   _____

4. _____

   _____

   _____

5. _____

_____

_____

6. _____

_____

_____

7. _____

_____

_____

Speak Out

Exercise 1   Choose a partner for this activity. Together, select a situation from the following list and think of two characters (one for each of you to play) who might find themselves in this situation. Then, from the second list, select a tone of voice for each character for a brief dialogue. You and your partner may choose the same tone of voice or different ones. Or you may choose a tone of voice that is not on the list.

Situations

1. the birth of a baby
2. a child's first day at school
3. a child skipping class
4. a child pretending to be sick so he or she won't have to go to school
5. graduating from school
6. cheating on an exam
7. being interviewed for a job
8. getting offered a job you don't want
9. getting fired
10. retiring
11. falling in love with someone who doesn't love you
12. getting divorced
13. getting married
14. changing careers
15. becoming a widow or widower

Tones of Voice

1. sad	8. hurt	15. nervous
2. angry	9. vengeful	16. passionate
3. depressed	10. shy	17. confused
4. delighted	11. sarcastic	18. envious
5. excited	12. guilty	19. mean
6. frightened	13. powerless	20. amused
7. loving	14. powerful	

Your character may talk about anything appropriate to the situation you've selected. To practice introducing negative comments, your characters should: (1) freely express negative opinions or facts and (2) try to use at least three expressions for introducing negative remarks. If time permits, choose another situation for the same characters and tones of voice or think of new characters and tones of voice and begin again.

Here is a sample dialogue for Situation 1, the birth of a baby. Terry speaks in a depressed tone, and Francis is amused.

Terry: Did you hear what happened after Jennifer's baby was born?

Francis: No! What happened?

Terry: Well, after seeing the baby, Jennifer's husband went home and cried.

Francis: You're kidding! Why?

Terry: Well, to put it bluntly, their baby is really ugly. Isn't that depressing?

Francis: No, not particularly. Let's face it: All newborn babies are ugly.

Terry: To tell the truth, I agree with you. It's a wonder more fathers don't go home and cry after they see their babies for the first time.

Francis: Well, why waste tears so soon? By the time they're teenagers, the parents will really have reasons to cry!

Exercise 2 With your partner, present a dialogue to the rest of the class, but do not tell your classmates which situation or emotions you have selected. After you've finished, let them guess.

CHAPTER 6
THE MIND

are four states of mind or consciousness: the waking state,
reaming state, the state of dreamless sleep, and an altered
of consciousness, a meditative state that is beyond the other
and is associated with profound spiritual experience. Does
these states represent reality? How can a person choose?
rofound spiritual experience—one that, by definition, tells
vhat you and the world really are—less real than your
ry waking hours? And what about dreams? How real are
The lecture in this chapter presents some provocative ideas
subject of dreams.

e: Dreams and Reality

Skill A: Listening for Comparisons

Skill B: Expressing the Positive View

PART ONE

DISCUSSION

As a class or in small groups, discuss the following:

1. Do you usually remember your dreams?

2. When do you remember your dreams? In other words, what
   circumstances do you associate with remembering your dreams?
   Do you remember them when you've eaten a large meal the
   night before, for example? Or had a stressful day? Or seen a
   dramatic movie?

3. Do you believe your dreams help you cope with daily life? If
   so, how?

4. Have you ever had a dream come true? For example, have you
   ever dreamed about getting lucky and later won a scholarship,
   received an unexpected gift, or had a chance meeting with
   someone who gave you good advice? Or have you ever dreamed
   of an accident that later occurred? Share your stories with your
   classmates.

VOCABULARY

Exercise 1 You may already know the meanings of some of
the following words. However, the words you know may be
different from the ones your classmates know. Working together,
match the definitions on the right with the words on the left.

74

Le Libérateur by
René Magritte.

1. __e__ chaotic
   /keɑtɪk/
2. __d__ to cling
3. __j__ conceptualization
4. __f__ fleeting
5. __c__ flexibility
6. __h__ to manipulate
7. __g__ perception
8. __a__ trivial
9. __i__ in tune with
10. __b__ visualization

a. unimportant, ordinary

b. formation of mental images

c. ability to bend; ability to adjust to new situations

d. to hold on tightly

e. disorderly, in a state of confusion

f. vanishing quickly

g. insight gained through the senses; observation

h. to manage (people, numbers, stocks, and so forth) skillfully for one's own profit

i. in harmony with, in agreement with

j. formation of theories, ideas, or concepts

Exercise 2 Replace the italicized words in the following telephone conversation with the appropriate vocabulary words from the left column in Exercise 1.

Practice Reading

conceptualization

fleeting
chaotic
perception
trivial
visualization
cling

flexibility

manipulate

in tune with

Stacy: Hi, Hank. What's up?

Hank: The most interesting thing is the topic we're covering in my psych course right now.

Stacy: What's that?

Hank: It's a unit on dreams.

Stacy: What's so interesting about dreams?

Hank: Well, for one thing, it's hard to come up with new theories about dreams. The *making of theories* is difficult because there are so many current theories.

Stacy: Like what?

Hank: Well, for one thing, there's the theory that dreams reflect reality.

Stacy: What do you mean by that?

Hank: Some philosophers argue that there is no way to prove that those *quickly disappearing* images we have in our sleep may be just another form of this crazy, *unorganized* world we live in. Our *view* of the world, which we get through sight, sound, touch, taste, and smell, may actually be changed through dreams.

Stacy: That sounds like it might not be *unimportant.* What else did you learn?

Hank: Well, that in some cultures the *formation of an image* that comes in a dream is considered to be no different from reality. And people in those cultures *hold on* so strongly to this belief that they react in waking life as though the dream were true. They seem to have no *willingness to adjust or change their minds* on this matter. For example, a Zulu man reportedly broke off a friendship after he dreamt that his friend intended to harm him.

Stacy: I wonder how that would work in our culture. People would try to *control and guide* their dreams so they could make their waking hours happier, don't you think?

Hank: I guess so. You'd really have to understand the workings of the mind to be so *in harmony with* your dreams like that, wouldn't you?

Stacy: Yeah, I guess you would.

Hank: Hey, listen. Enough about school. You want to catch a movie Thursday night?

Stacy: Sure. What did you have in mind?

Hank: Renoir's *The Grand Illusion* is playing at the Fine Arts. Want to see it?

Stacy: Sure, come by for me at 6:00.

Hank: Okay, see you then. 'Bye.

Stacy: 'Bye.

PART TWO

SKILL A: LISTENING FOR COMPARISONS AND CONTRASTS

In the previous chapter, you learned about using analogies for comparison—that is, looking at the similarities between two things. English speakers commonly use analogies both in formal and informal situations. For example, in a lecture on the nature of dreams, you might hear an analogy such as, "Dreams are like smoke. You can't quite get ahold of them, and they go away so quickly that you can barely remember them." Or in a conversation, a friend might say, "In my dream last night the clouds were like human heads, each one smiling and wearing a funny hat. I woke up laughing."

Another way you can look at the relationship between two things is by pointing out their differences, that is, by *contrasting* them. *Comparison and contrast* occur when the similarities and differences between two items are looked at together. Speakers who are comparing speak about the likenesses between people or things and usually try to show:

How is X like Y?
Which aspects of X and Y can be compared?

Speakers who are contrasting talk about the differences between people or things and try to show:

How is X different from Y?

Comparisons and contrasts are used frequently to call the listener's attention to characteristics or points that might otherwise be overlooked. The speaker believes the listener would not otherwise make the connections between certain characteristics or points and thus uses comparisons or contrasts to specify these connections. Because comparison and contrast are used so frequently, it is important for you to recognize them.

Comparison and contrast can be indicated in three main ways: (1) with words that signal comparison or contrast, (2) with antonyms (words with opposite meanings), and (3) with intonation.

1. Here are some words that signal comparison.

again	likewise
also	similarly
and so does	the same way (as)
equally important	too
in a like manner	

77

And here are some words that signal contrast.

although/though	nevertheless
but	on the contrary
by (in) contrast	on the other hand
conversely	whereas
however	yet
meanwhile	

2. Antonyms can be used to show contrast when the speaker is talking about one topic or idea.

Fortunately . . . Unfortunately . . .
The advantages are . . . The disadvantages are . . .
The positive features are . . . The negative features are . . .
The best part is . . . The worst part is . . .

3. Word stress and intonation can also indicate comparison and contrast. For example, in the following sentences, comparison is indicated by stressing the words *mind* and *body* and by using a slightly rising intonation on the first sentence and a slightly falling intonation on the second sentence. Try it.

The *mind* repairs itself during sleep.
The *body* repairs itself during sleep.

The following conversations show examples of informal use of comparison and contrast.

Conversation 1

Otto: I like the German restaurant on Second Street.
Henry: I've never been there. Why do you like it?
Otto: They cook food the same way my mother did when she was alive. It makes me dream about my childhood.

Conversation 2

Judy: Should we drive or take the train to the concert in Chicago?
Paula: Well, let's see, if we drive, we can leave whenever we want. On the other hand, if we take the train, we don't have to worry about parking and we can sleep on the train on the way home and dream about you know who!

Conversation 3

T.A.:   What do you want first, the good news or the bad news?
(Voices of students)
T.A.:   The good news is there's no quiz about the mind today in class.
(Voices of students)

T.A.: The bad news is that this means that next week we'll have *two* quizzes, one on the mind in a waking state on Thursday and one on the mind in a dreaming state on Friday.

Listen In

Exercise 1 The following chart lists some of the comparisons and contrasts given in the lecture. Listen to the lecture once to get the main ideas and organizational pattern. Then listen again, this time focusing on the comparisons and contrasts. Fill in the chart as you listen, replaying the tape as often as necessary. You may wish to practice using abbreviations. The first item has been done for you.

COMPARISONS AND CONTRASTS: DREAMS AND REALITY

	Comparison	Contrast
1. Dreams and waking life	*Inspirations in science and art can come from images in dreams or waking life.*	*Dream images are more subtle than images when one is awake.*
2. Two types of dreams		

79

COMPARISONS AND CONTRASTS: DREAMS AND REALITY

	Comparison	Contrast
3. Dr. Haber's reaction to George and other people's reaction to George		_____ _____ _____ _____ _____ _____ _____
4. George and Dr. Haber	_____ _____ _____ _____ _____ _____ _____	_____ _____ _____ _____ _____ _____ _____
5. The lathe of heaven and a child playing with a tape recorder	_____ _____ _____ _____ _____ _____ _____	

	Comparison	Contrast
6. Our concept of time and Le Guin's concept of time		

Exercise 2   Listen to the lecture and write any words you hear that might signal a comparison or contrast.

_____

_____

_____

_____

_____

_____

_____

_____

Hand with Reflecting Globe by M. C. Escher.

Are there any comparisons or contrasts in the lecture that are not signaled by these words? If so, what let you know that some things were being compared or contrasted? Are there any comparisons or contrasts shown by intonation? Discuss your responses with your classmates.

Speak Out

Exercise 1   Le Guin's suggestion that reality cannot be fixed or held still in order to be controlled was pointed out in the lecture. Similarly, our dreams cannot be held still or controlled, which may be one reason we can learn about our true hopes, beliefs, and

Time Transfixed by René Magritte.

feelings from our dreams. Some dreams are symbolic; others are more straightforward representations of actual events. In the following activity, you will compare and contrast two dreams that are triggered by the same event. For each one, first read the situation and the two dreams. Then discuss as a class:

1. How are the dreams similar?

2. How are the dreams different?

3. Which one is more symbolic and which one is more related to actual events? Why?

Situation 1: You and a friend read the following story in a newspaper: The Hotel Ritz has been robbed. Three professional gunmen, posing as doctors, entered the hotel in Dallas. Because there was a medical convention in the hotel at the time, the gunmen were undetected and made a clean getaway.

Dream 1: A doctor is examining you, but instead of being in an office, you are in your car. All of a sudden, the doctor pulls out a gun.

Dream 2: You have invited a few friends for dinner. You are making the final preparations in the kitchen. As you reach for the butter, it turns into a pistol.

Situation 2: The atmosphere at school has been chaotic because final examinations will be given next week. Of course, students are frantically studying. You're especially worried about your economics final because your instructor is hard to understand and reminds you of a rhinoceros.

Dream 1: While you are in the library with your economics book, you notice a giraffe chewing a textbook on the table next to yours. Nobody but you seems to notice.

Dream 2: You are reading a paperback in bed with your stereo blaring. Everything is fine. All at once, your normally well-behaved dog jumps on the bed and begins howling and will not stop. Even hitting him with your book will not quiet your frantic pet.

Situation 3: A quarrel between two men in the office stems from administrative policies. Jim, who has worked there longer, wants the promotion, but the offer was made to Michael, a newer employee who has been working for Jim. No seniority system exists.

Jim's dream: A rock band is playing in the cafeteria, and everyone is eating pink and green food with stars on it. Jim asks the band to play some folk music, but the band members ignore him. He tries to buy some of the pink and green food with stars on it, but the young man at the cash register says he's too old to eat this food and asks him to leave.

Michael's dream: Michael has a conversation with Jim and apologizes for the argument. Jim forgives him and announces that he has a new job at twice the salary at a Japanese company just opening down the street.

Situation 4: You have read in the newspaper of a group of skiers who have been missing for two weeks. Rescue teams fear the worst because avalanches have been occurring daily this winter.

Dream 1: You are jogging in shorts and a T-shirt. The weather changes drastically, and it begins to rain. To make matters worse, you are eight miles from home.

Dream 2: You are walking in the snow thinking about how fresh and clear the air is. Your warm clothing feels too heavy and tight all of a sudden. Soon you are having trouble breathing. Your hat keeps falling down over your eyes, and your collar creeps up over your mouth. You wake up gasping for air.

Situation 5: Tom reads in the paper that since it is the last Sunday in October, he must set his clock back one hour.

Dream 1: He dreams that he wakes up in the morning and everything is backwards. He walks backwards to the bathroom to brush his teeth and sees the back of his head in the mirror. He feels like he is putting on his clothing correctly, but when he looks down it is all backwards. The car goes in reverse to work, and at the end of the day when he climbs into bed he finds his head where his feet usually rest.

Dream 2: Tom dreams that he is an hour early for a major appointment with a man named Mr. Timekeeper. Mr. Timekeeper is very impressed that Tom is so early and gives Tom four million dollars' worth of business.

Exercise 2 In this activity, you will have an opportunity to further try your hand at dream analysis. Form small groups, then put on your glasses and wrinkle your brow, for you have been appointed to serve with a team of psychoanalysts who must analyze the dreams of the following patients. As a team, decide how the dreams are alike and how they are different. Are they related to one major issue, or do they represent different issues in the life of the dreamer/patient?

Patient 1: Peter is a thirty-eight-year-old used-car salesman who has recently filed for bankruptcy. His wife has threatened to leave him unless he gets out of debt.

Dream 1: He jumps off the Eiffel Tower but is picked up by a stork and carried to the Caribbean.

Dream 2: He is at his bank making a night deposit when two female outlaws hold up the bank and leave him tied up and bound with a scarf so that he cannot talk.

Dream 3: He flies to Italy to order lasagna, but can find only pizza. As he enjoys the pizza, a helicopter lands across the street and two men get out and offer him $77,000.

Patient 2: Martin, from Denver, Colorado, marries Françoise, from Lyon, France, and lives and works in Lyon for three years. Then they move back to Denver.

Dream 1: Martin dreams he is back in Lyon at their apartment talking to the neighbors.

Dream 2: Martin dreams he is alone in an airplane, and all the signs and control indicators are labeled in French. He picks up an equipment manual, which is written in French, and realizes he can't read it.

Dream 3: Martin goes to the office in Denver and finds that all of the people there are his co-workers from France. None of them speaks English, and all of them need his help. He speaks French perfectly and easily arranges housing for his co-workers. When he finishes, everyone cheers and they pick him up on their shoulders and carry him around the office.

Patient 3: An elderly man, Mr. Hill, describes these dreams.

Dream 1: Mr. Hill dreams he is in college taking courses and living in the dorms. Although he does very well, no one notices or sees him.

Dream 2: Mr. Hill is a young man working on his father's ranch. Everyone is looking at the blue sky and hoping for rain.

Dream 3: Mr. Hill meets his first grandchildren. They are twins, a boy and a girl. The boy looks like him and the girl looks like his deceased wife.

Patient 4: Tina is a freshman at Santa Barbara City College, majoring in computer science.

Dream 1: Tina is in a computer store selecting a word processor. As she walks up to look at one, it changes into an ice cream sundae. The second one changes into a bicycle, the third into a small swimming pool, the fourth into a refrigerator, and the fifth into a sculpture of a dancer. She leaves the store feeling worried that she'll never find a computer that will stick around.

Dream 2: Tina walks into class feeling very good, confident about the exam she is about to take. She sits down, and the instructor passes out the exam. She takes one look at it and can't remember anything.

Dream 3: Tina is at a party and three men come up to her and ask her to dance. She can't decide whom to dance with.

Exercise 3 Ask three people outside of class who are native speakers of English about a dream they remember or a recurring dream they've had. Find out as much as you can about each dream. Share your findings with your classmates. Do you think anyone could have had these dreams or only a native speaker of English? Why?

SKILL B: EXPRESSING THE POSITIVE VIEW

Often in everyday life, people find themselves in situations where they are listening to colleagues, friends, or acquaintances who are complaining about something that has gone wrong at work, school, home, with a business, or at a shop. To console the unhappy person, the listener suggests ways to look at the problem as though it were "all for the best." This ability to look at the "bright" or optimistic side of an issue can be a good skill to have, not only in informal situations, but also during more formal discussions.

Quite often expressions used to signal contrasts, such as *on the other hand, nevertheless,* and *however* (see "Skill A" for a more complete list), are used to introduce an optimistic view that contrasts with a pessimistic one.

The following expressions are also used frequently (especially in more informal situations with topics of a personal nature) to express the positive side of a situation.

> Yes, but just think . . .
> Yes, that's true, but . . .
> Well, try to look at it this way . . .
> It's all for the best, because . . .
> Well, look at the bright side . . .
> But, on the bright side . . .
> Well, at least . . .

Another way to present the positive side of a negative situation or idea is to make the situation or idea seem more tolerable by comparing it with another situation or idea (usually hypothetical) that is even worse.

> Yes, but it (things) could be worse! What if . . .
> Just imagine if . . .

Listen to the following conversations.

Conversation 1

Gary: Hi Julius. How's it going?
Julius: Hi Gary. I'm really tired. I didn't sleep much last night because I had this terrible dream. I dreamed that I got the second-to-the-lowest grade on the history final.

Gary: Oh yeah? And who got the *lowest* grade?

Julius: Henry Mitchell. Gee—what a horrible dream!

Gary: Well, it could have been worse.

Julius: Yeah? How?

Gary: Well, you could have awakened and discovered you *were* Henry Mitchell.

Conversation 2

Christine: Oh shoot! It's raining again, and I was looking forward to going to the soccer team picnic.

Eric: Yeah—too bad—but look at it this way. Now we'll have time to go see that hypnotherapist I was telling you about.

Christine: Oh, well—maybe . . .

Eric: Now come on, you said you wanted to stop smoking, didn't you?

Conversation 3

Clara: Hi, Joyce. What's up?

Joyce: Hi, Clara. I'm on my way over to my study skills class. We're starting a unit on speed-reading, and I'm not looking forward to it.

Clara: Really? Why not?

Joyce: Well, I'm afraid that those speed-reading techniques might interfere with my reading comprehension. And I already have so much trouble understanding a lot of the material in my classes.

Clara: Well, look at the bright side. You'll learn to read everything so quickly that you'll at least read everything once. You *were* having trouble completing all of the reading assignments on time, weren't you?

Joyce: Yes, but remember what the comedian Woody Allen said a speed-reading course did for him?

Clara: No—what?

Joyce: He said: "Well, after the speed-reading course I really improved. I was able to read Tolstoy's *War and Peace* in five minutes. . . . Yes—it's about war."

Listen In

Exercise 1   The following ten items (Exercise 2) have been either paraphrased or taken word for word from the lecture. Each of the items describes something that might be seen as negative or unpleasant. Listen to the lecture. Listen for the parts in the lecture that correspond to these items. Also listen for any information given in the lecture that provides counterarguments, or the "bright side."

Exercise 2 Listen to the lecture once again or several more times if necessary. This time write down the positive side of each item in the spaces provided. When the lecturer uses an expression listed in "Skill B" to introduce the bright side, write down that item as well (Items 2, 3, 4, and 7, marked with asterisks). When the instructor does not use one of these expressions to introduce the bright side, choose one of your own to introduce your own positive statement. Remember that some of the items paraphrase parts of the lecture. Some of your positive comments may have to be paraphrases as well. The first two have been done for you. Compare your answers with your classmates'.

1. Dreams are very mysterious.

    Yes, but look at it this way: It's these kinds of mysteries that make life interesting.

2. Dreams can be irrelevant to waking life, even silly.

    * *On the other hand, many breakthroughs in science and inspirations in the arts came through dreams.*

3. After Coleridge's writing was interrupted by a visitor, he could not remember the rest of the poem he had created in a dream.

    * _____

    _____

    _____

4. And one night last week I dreamed about hot dogs piled up on a bridge—no useful images for scientific discoveries or artistic creations there that I can figure out.

    * _____

    _____

    _____

5. Every time George dreams a new reality, each person in the world forgets who they once were and acquires a new set of memories to fit this new reality.

    _____

    _____

    _____

6. Dr. Haber has been trying to use George's dreams to change the world.

_____

_____

_____

7. Dr. Haber dreams that everything is gray—the people, the buildings, the animals, and the plants.

* _____

_____

_____

8. Time is moved forward or backward in response to George's dreams.

_____

_____

_____

Speak Out

Exercise 1   When you are involved in either a formal debate or an informal discussion of a particular topic, you may find yourself taking one side of the issue or the other. You may be for or against, pro or con. Sometimes you may state the advantages or disadvantages in a moderate manner. At other times, you may want to take an extremely optimistic or pessimistic view and strongly present either the positive or negative aspects of the particular issue. In this exercise, you will have the opportunity to be the eternal optimist who sees the bright side of everything and the immovable pessimist who sees only the negative, as you participate in debates on the topics in the following list.

Divide into teams of three to six persons. Form a group with another team and together select a topic from the list. Decide which team will present the optimistic view of the topic and which team will present the pessimistic view. Then, as a team, take five to ten minutes to plan your strategy for the debate. Imagine what the other team's arguments will be and then come up with as many counterarguments as you can (either the positive or the negative, depending on which side your team is representing). After a few minutes of preparation, begin the debate. Even if the moderate view seems the most reasonable one, try to stick to your role as the eternal optimist or immovable pessimist during the debate.

Take turns with the members of the opposing team presenting

arguments and counterarguments. If you are presenting the positive side, use expressions listed in "Skill B" in this chapter to emphasize your points. If you are presenting the negative side, you might want to refer to the expressions listed in "Skill B," Chapter 5. You may want to have your instructor or a classmate serve as a moderator and give points for each good argument presented.

When you have finished the debate, choose another topic, change roles with the opposing team (for example, take the side of the pessimist this time if you were on the side of the optimist in the first debate), prepare as before, and then begin the debate. Debate as many of the topics in this way as time allows. You may want to debate other teams for variety.

Topics

1. hypnosis
2. mind-altering drugs such as LSD
3. telepathy
4. memorization as a method of study
5. many years of intense study on a particular subject, excluding all other areas of study
6. controlling anger at all times
7. being totally honest at all times
8. daydreaming
9. treatment of mental illness with drugs
10. experimenting with mind-altering situations such as sleep deprivation or total sensory deprivation

Exercise 2 Sometimes when you're discussing something, you may become very negative, especially if you're discussing an ongoing problem that is extremely irritating or that you think can't be solved. If the other people in the conversation have similar feelings about the particular topic under discussion, they might join in and add a few of their own complaints. A conversation that degenerates into one complaint after the other is called a "gripe session" (*gripe* means "complaint"). A gripe session can be a good thing, because it lets you get your feelings out into the open, thus clearing the air of any tension caused by hidden feelings. It may even let you get a little sympathy and commiseration from those who feel the same way. Sometimes, however, a gripe session goes on too long, becoming extremely negative and producing no positive solutions to a problem. This is the time when the eternal optimist, the person who sees the bright side of the situation, is most welcome. In this activity, you will have the opportunity to have a gripe session on a topic of your choice and to help everyone to see the bright side.

In small groups, choose a topic for discussion. (Some possibilities are given in the following list.) Then complain all you want. If you have no complaints or if you have already stated the ones you have, try to offer the optimistic view, the bright side, whenever someone else complains.

When you have exhausted your complaints about the first topic you chose and have countered them with the positive side (probably after a few minutes), choose another topic and begin again. Cover as many different topics as time permits.

Suggested Topics

1. dormitory or cafeteria food
2. bureaucracies/red tape
3. politicians/politics
4. traffic/parking
5. roommates
6. single life/married life
7. final exams/writing papers
8. going to the dentist
9. . . . music/ . . . art
10. people who . . .
11. the high cost of . . .
12. the quality of . . .

CHAPTER 7
WORKING

Think about the cars on American streets and highways. Even though the drivers live in America, many of them choose to buy Japanese cars. The astounding success of Japanese automobiles, computers, televisions, and other products alarms many American corporate executives.

How did these Japanese companies become so successful so quickly? Are they more efficient and productive than American companies? Are the workers in Japan treated differently from American workers? What can American corporations do to compete with imported Japanese products? These and other questions will be considered in the lecture in this chapter.

Lecture: Japanese and American Systems of Management
Skill A: Listening for Causes and Effects
Skill B: Persuading and "Giving In"

PART ONE

DISCUSSION

What images does the term *work* bring to your mind? Do you envision bored people sweating on an assembly line, watching the clock? Or do you picture an excited group of people working cooperatively on a project that will profit all of them?

Because most of us will be working most of our lives, it is useful to clarify our attitudes toward work. The following questions are designed to give you a chance to hear your classmates' attitudes toward work and to clarify your own. Answer the questions in small groups.

1. Have you or anyone you know ever had a job that you thought was wonderful? What made it so good?

2. Have you or anyone you know ever had a terrible job? What made it so bad?

3. What do you think the "perfect job" would be? Create a fantasy job in your mind and share it with your group. What is it? Where is it? What are the hours? How much do you earn? With whom do you work?

4. Under what conditions do you think it is important for workers to cooperate and rely on each other? Under what conditions is an interdependent work situation better than one in which each person does a separate task?

5. Each person has a slightly different definition of job satisfaction. Read the items in the following list and rank them from

1 to 10 (1 is for the most important and 10 is the least important) according to your criteria of job satisfaction. If you have nothing to specify for the category *other*, rank the categories from 1 to 9. Compare your answers with your classmates'. What category did most people rank first? What category did most people rank last?

_____ mental challenge

_____ good pay

_____ health and hospital care

_____ long paid vacations

_____ opportunities for advancement

_____ individual recognition

_____ flexible working hours

_____ cooperative decision making involving both worker and management

_____ friendly co-workers

_____ other

VOCABULARY

Exercise 1 Some of you may already know the meanings of several of the following words. However, the words you know may be different from the ones your classmates know. Pool your knowledge and match the definitions on the right with the words on the left.

1. _b_ to assemble
2. _f_ consensus
3. _g_ consultant
4. _c_ dispute
5. _d_ imperative
6. _a_ individualism
7. _e_ innovation
8. _i_ interdependence
9. _j_ to slump
10. _h_ quota

a. the belief that the interests of the individual should take precedence over the interests of the group
b. to put together
c. disagreement
d. necessary, mandatory
e. newly introduced idea, method, or device
f. collective opinion 輿論
g. person who gives expert advice in a particular field
h. maximum number (especially of people allowed to enter a place)
i. mutual reliance or support
j. to fall or sink suddenly

Exercise 2 Fill in the blanks with the appropriate forms of the words from the vocabulary list.

93

American companies often find themselves in economic trouble. Their stockholders become uneasy, and quick action is imperative. It is common practice for specialists or consultants to be called in to help find a solution to the company's problem. In fact, this has just occurred at a major corporation. A _consultant_ has been hired by XYZ to find out why sales have _slumped_ in recent months. In order to learn more about the company's problems the consultant has arranged a meeting with company managers. This consultant believes that it is _imperative_ that he understand the existing philosophy before he introduces any _innovations_ or makes any changes.

According to the company philosophy, each worker is expected to take the initiative on a new idea; workers are not led by the hand. However, once the individual devises the idea, a _consensus_ or collective agreement is needed before the idea can be carried out. Once there is agreement about an idea, costs are carefully analyzed to judge whether the idea fits with the general plan. Then, if the project is determined to be worthy of company effort, a team is _assembled_. This cooperation or _interdependence_ among workers makes the company's managers proud. The company's cooperative policies have been working well up until the past few months; workers have been content, and few _disputes_ have occurred among the workers. Because the working conditions are so favorable, the sales slump must be caused by other factors. At least that is the assumption the consultant will start with.

PART TWO

SKILL A: LISTENING FOR CAUSES AND EFFECTS

When businesspeople and researchers look at successful companies, they often ask themselves: What factors make the company successful? To answer the question, they examine various factors to decide which ones seem to be related. Then they determine if the relationship is one of cause and effect rather than mere coincidence. For example, one automobile dealership sells more Oldsmobiles than any other Oldsmobile dealer. The other dealers wonder why. They look at many factors: location of the showroom, business hours, prices of the cars, and the amount of commission paid to salespeople. When the dealers discover that the showroom location of each dealership is similar, the business hours are similar, and the prices of the cars are similar, but that the commission paid to the salespeople is greater at the most successful dealerships, they suspect a cause-and-effect relationship.

Seeing cause-and-effect relationships can help us find solutions to problems in all aspects of life, from business to academic life, from social situations to solitary ones. It's not surprising, therefore, that instructors present causes and effects as they lecture. In explaining cause-and-effect relationships, lecturers generally use two approaches. Method 1 is a straightforward approach. The instructor explicitly states, "Here is the cause and here is the effect," or some variation of this sentence. Method 2 is a less obvious approach. Causes and effects are presented as a series of facts with implied connections rather than explicitly stated ones, and it is the student's job to recognize the implications and to make the connections.

If a lecturer uses Method 1, you may find the best note-taking system is to put all the causes on one side of a page and all the effects on the opposite side. For example, here are some notes on the garbage collectors' strike in New York from a lecture on labor unions and management.

Causes	Effects
1a. low wages	1. workers strike
1b. long hours	
1c. dirty working conditions	
2. strike	2a. tourist business is lost
	2b. city looks ugly
	2c. areas smell bad
	2d. disease breaks out
3. picketers throw rocks at "scab" workers	3a. twenty-five persons are arrested
	3b. bad feelings increase between management and employees

If the lecturer uses Method 2, however, it may be more difficult to make the connection between causes and effects. If you don't catch on as you go along, keep taking notes to get down all the information. You can go back later and reread your notes to determine which bits of information are causes and which are effects. You can then show connections between causes and effects with numbers, arrows, or any other system you'd like to use.

Causes, effects, and their relationships are frequently signaled by the following expressions:

Expressions Signaling Causes

because
for
since

Expressions Signaling Effects

as a consequence
as a result
consequently
hence
so
therefore
thus

Expressions Signaling a Cause/Effect Relationship

as a consequence of . . .
as a result of . . .
due to the fact that
due to this
due to this fact
for this reason
if . . . then
when . . . then

Listen In

HOW WOULD <u>YOU</u> RUN A DOORBELL COMPANY?

---

1. Supervision of production; wages
   a. Use a supervisor. Have a supervisor record the number of doorbells each worker assembles; pay each person according to how many he or she produces.
   b. Don't use a supervisor, but do have a team of workers assemble the doorbells. Record the number of doorbells assembled by a production team of several workers without a supervisor and provide equal bonuses for each member of the team when more than a specific number is produced.

Workers doing their daily gymnastics at the Mitsubishi shipbuilding yard, Nagasaki, Japan.

2. Raises and promotions
   a. Give frequent raises and promotions to workers who work fastest. Give frequent raises and promotions to workers who work hardest. Give fewer rewards to the others.
   b. Give few but regular promotions and raises to everyone on the basis of age and number of years with the company.
3. Slow work periods
   a. Hire many workers during periods when the demand for doorbells is heavy; fire unnecessary workers when business slows down. Don't reduce pay of those who remain employed.
   b. Give all employees life-long employment guarantees. Reduce pay and hours for both labor and management, but fire no one when business slows down.

The assembly line at a Nissan Motors plant appears to be similar to assembly lines at American companies. So what's the secret?

4. Quality control
   a. Have an outside inspector responsible for quality control. The outside inspector is someone who is not involved in the production process.
   b. Make the work team responsible for quality control. Give extra money or time off for excellent records. Encourage team workmanship by giving awards and public praise.

5. Changes and improvements in the system
   a. Use outside consultants to get new ideas for improving electronic doorbells. Reward individual workers who make usable suggestions. To avoid disagreements among workers, let management decide on all changes.
   b. Use work teams to get new ideas. Have regular discussion meetings of the work team. Make changes slowly, only after workers and management agree.

Listen to the lecture once through. Then listen again. This time, take notes by filling in the accompanying chart listing causes and effects discussed in the lecture. Some of the information has been provided for you. Share your answers with your classmates.

Causes

1a. Japanese products are easy to get.

1b. Japanese products are

_____ .

1c. Japanese products are

_____ .

2. _____

_____

_____

3. _____

_____

_____

4. U.S. manager encourages individual initiative.

5. Japanese manager encourages group efforts.

6a. Japan is a small country.

6b. Japan is isolated.

6c. Japan is

_____ .

Effects

1. Americans buy many Japanese products.

2. American companies are losing business.

3a. Some leaders in business, labor, and government want protective taxes and

_____ .

3b. Other leaders say the United States should

_____ .

4a. Separate people moving up from

_____ .

4b. Keep clear division

between _____

_____ .

5a. _____

_____ .

5b. _____

_____ .

6. _____

_____

_____ .

Causes

Effects

7a. The United States is

_____

_____ .

7. Competitive business practices and unconventional business practices.

7b. The United States has

_____

_____ .

7c. The United States has

_____

_____ .

7d. The people in the United

States like _____

_____ .

8a. William Ouchi says the United States should strengthen the bond between workers and their companies by providing

_____

_____ ,

8b. _____

_____ ,

8c. _____

_____ ,

8d. and _____

_____ .

8a. Then United States productivity will

_____ .

8b. And in the long run, these reforms will bring

_____

_____ ,

8c. _____ ,

8d. _____ ,

8e. and _____ .

9a. IBM, Intel, Procter and Gamble, Hewlett-Packard

have _____

_____ ,

9b. _____

_____ ,

9c. and _____

_____ .

9a. Decrease in

_____

_____

9b. and _____ .

9c. Increase in

_____

9d. and _____ .

Causes	Effects	
10. U.S. companies adopt Japanese business philosophy.	10. U.S. citizens _____ _____ .	PART TWO

Speak Out

Exercise 1 The following items are available through mail-order catalogs in the United States. Each one represents a technological advance that has had a marked effect on our way of life. Can you think of or have you read about any other technological 'toys' that might have had an important effect on either individual lives or

Introducing the new Kodak Ektaprint 225 copier-duplicator.

Now you can make two-sided copies—from one- or two-sided originals—automatically. With the Ektaprint 225 copier, you needn't touch originals or copies until the job is done. Only the button that says "two-sided." Plus, there's a full array of advanced finishing capabilities: New slip sheeting puts colorful dividers anywhere in the set. New "chapterization" starts chapters on right-hand pages. And there's automatic in-line insertion of cover sheets or letterhead. But, for all that's new, it's all on the same proven-reliable mainframe. Call, or send the coupon. Availability limited.
1 800 44KODAK (1 800 445-6325) Ext. 324.

From beans to brew while you sleep.

My Café by Toshiba is the first automatic drip coffee system in the world with a coffee mill built right into the brew basket. Pour in whole beans and set the digital timer before you go to bed. In the morning, wake up to the aroma of freshly ground and brewed coffee.

10-function panel controls clock, 24-hour timer, coffee strength (light or dark), bean mill time (0–20 secs.), and two hour "keep warm" feature. Brews pre-ground coffee too. 1 to 8 cups capacity. High-impact, heat-resistant plastic body with glass carafe, built-in stainless steel filter.

One year warranty. Call now for the freshest, most flavorful coffee you've ever brewed.
• Toshiba My Café #ETS316 $129 (4.50)

ORDER TOLL-FREE, 24 HRS. EVERY DAY.
800 344-4444
Canadian overseas orders 415-344-4444
Toll free ordering by credit card only.

society as a whole? Look in some current popular magazines, mail-order catalogs, and business or scientific journals. Cut out or copy a few pictures and descriptions of your favorite items. Bring them to class and use them to do this activity.

In small groups, look at each picture and read the descriptions aloud. Then discuss these questions.

1. In what ways is such a device beneficial? To whom?
2. Could this item have a major effect on our lives? If so, would it be a positive or negative effect?
3. Which of these items would cause the most dramatic effect on society as a whole? Why do you think so?

Exercise 2   In small groups, share your answers to the following questions.

1. If you could design something the average household needs, what would it be? Describe it.
2. How would it affect society as a whole?

Share a few of the most beneficial or most imaginative ideas of the class.

SKILL B: PERSUADING AND "GIVING IN"

The most effective way to persuade someone to come over to your point of view is to present a strong argument. A persuasive argument may appeal either to the reason or to the emotions of the listener, but in both cases it will have its own logic. That is, reasons will be given as to why this particular argument or point of view is a good one. Often these reasons are essentially statements of cause-and-effect relationships. For example, someone might say:

More companies in this country should adopt Japanese-style management practices. A company in my town did this and doubled both productivity and sales.

To be even more persuasive, you can give additional reasons. Often the more points you make in favor of your argument, the more likely you are to persuade the listener. For example, let's continue the argument:

Not only that, but the employees are much happier, so they are generally healthier and don't have to take so many days off because of illness. What's more, the food in the employee cafeteria is really terrific, so the employees don't have to eat in expensive restaurants or take time to make their own lunches.

When you are trying to be persuasive, you can use expressions that emphasize the fact that you are about to make further points to the argument, that you are adding statements that you hope will influence the listener. Following are some of the most common expressions used to strengthen arguments by giving additional reasons:

Along with that . . .
And another thing . . .
And I might add . . .
Besides . . .
Furthermore . . .
In addition (to that) . . .
Not only that, but . . .
Not to mention the fact that . . .
Moreover . . .
Plus the fact that . . .
What's more . . .

Most of these expressions are straightforward and clear, but one may seem confusing to you at first. When you use the expression "Not to mention the fact that . . . ," you *will*, of course, mention the point that the expression—if interpreted literally—indicates that you will *not* mention. The expression is an idiom, difficult to interpret literally, but it is used in the same manner as the other expressions in the list.

Now what do you say when someone has managed to persuade you to come over to his or her point of view and "give in"? How can you let this person know that you think he or she has presented a convincing argument? Following are some of the most common expressions used to "give in":

> (I guess) You're right (after all).
> (I guess) You've convinced me.
> If you really insist.
> I'll buy that.
> I'll go along with that.
> I'm sold.
> Maybe you're right.
> Perhaps in this case (you're right).
> You may have a point there. (You've got a point there.)
> You've sold me.

These expressions are appropriate in most situations. The only time they would not be appropriate is when the speaker is clearly an authority on the subject and the arguments are not being presented for the purpose of persuasion.

Persuading and giving in do not take place only during intellectual discussions. For instance, at some time you may want to persuade someone to actually *do* something, not to just agree with your point of view. In that case, you can persuade by offering an incentive or positive consequence. For example, consider this offer made to a fellow employee:

> Could you help me out? I'd really like to go to San Francisco for the weekend, but I've been scheduled to work on Saturday. Will you fill in for me on Saturday if I work for you on the day you want to take off to visit your mother?

When you have been persuaded because of an enticing offer, you can give in by using one of the following expressions:

> Come to think of it . . .
> If you insist . . .
> I'm sold!
> In that case . . .
> Now that you mention it . . .
> On second thought . . .
> That's an offer I can't refuse!
> You've sold me!
> You've talked me into it.
> When you put it that way . . .

You can also persuade someone to do something by presenting the negative consequences that will result if the person does not do what you are asking. For example:

> Do you think you could work on Saturday? If we all don't work some extra time this week, we won't get this project finished and the company might lose the contract.

When you have been persuaded because of negative consequences, you can give in by using one of these expressions:

Given that there seems to be (I've got no, there's no) choice . . .
If I absolutely have to . . .
If that's the only alternative . . .
If that's the only way . . .
If that's the way it's got to be . . .
If there's no other alternative . . .
If there's no other way . . .
If you insist . . .
Okay, just this once (one time).
That's an offer I guess I'd better not refuse!
Well, under those circumstances . . .

Notice that a few of the expressions such as "I'm sold" and "if you insist" appear on more than one of the lists for giving in, as they are appropriate in more than one type of situation.

Listen to the following conversation, which involves persuading and giving in. A Japanese corporate executive is trying to persuade local government officials to allow the Japanese company to build a factory in their town in the United States.

Executive: Our company is one of the most successful of its kind in Japan. We are sure to be successful here as well.
Official 1:   That will be good for your company, but exactly how will it help our town?
Executive: Well, first of all, we will hire only local people to work in the factory.
Official 1:   Does that include all the employees? Even those in management positions?
Executive: Yes, for the most part. We will, of course, have some of our personnel from Japan in management positions to get things started and to teach our management system.
Official 1:   That sounds good. Now what about your waste products? What will you do about them? We don't want any industrial waste problems here!
Executive: There really isn't any waste to speak of. Not only that, the industry is very quiet as well. So you will have no noise pollution from us.
Official 1:   I'm sold. It sounds like an ideal situation. How about you, mayor? What do you think?
Mayor: Well, I'd like to know more about your management system. I'm not so sure the people in our town will be happy with that system, not to mention the fact that I have my doubts about how well your product will sell over here.
Executive: You may have a point there. But our company is

willing to take that chance. What's more, if the management system does prove to be unsatisfactory, we're willing to modify it as necessary to keep the employees satisfied and to keep our production rate up. And I might add that our company is willing to pay top dollar to the city for the use of that land by the railroad tracks where we want to build our factory.

Mayor: I see. In that case, you've talked me into it!

Listen In

Exercise 1   Listen to the lecture again. As you listen, make a list of the expressions the lecturer uses to give additional reasons and thereby persuade you to agree with certain ideas. Then compare your list with your classmates'.

_____

_____

_____

_____

_____

_____

Japanese-style loyalty to the company is catching on at General Electric.

Exercise 2 Clearly, the lecturer has a particular point of view. In one or two sentences, state what you think the lecturer's point of view is. Did the lecturer persuade you to agree with this point of view? Why or why not? Share your answers with your class-mates.

_____

_____

_____

Exercise 3 Listen to the conversations in "Skill B" again. Jot down any persuasive points made by the speakers. Which speakers give in and which expressions do they use to indicate this? Again, share your responses.

_____

_____

_____

_____

_____

_____

_____

Speak Out

Exercise 1 As a class or in smaller groups, form teams to represent opposing sides in debates on work-related issues. Choose from the following topics or devise your own topics for debate. Use the techniques and expressions described in "Skill B" to persuade your opponents to accept your point of view and to give in each time they present a convincing argument.

1. Trade unions are/are not the best means of solving problems in the workplace.
2. Industrial spying is/is not justifiable.
3. White-collar jobs should/should not have more prestige than blue-collar jobs.
4. Women should/should not be allowed to do *any* job they choose if they meet the basic qualifications.
5. Robots in the workplace are a help/hindrance to the welfare of workers.

6. Management should/should not involve itself in the personal life and well-being of its employees.

7. Selecting children at a young age and training them for certain professions is/is not best for these individuals and for society as a whole.

8. Companies should/should not be responsible for the costs of continuing education for employees even if such education is not directly related to their work.

9. All employees should/should not be given at least one year paid leave of absence during their careers to do whatever they wish.

Exercise 2 In pairs, choose one of the following scenarios to role-play. Use the expressions for persuading and giving in as your characters express their views to each other. If time permits, change partners one or more times and do the activity again. Then present one of the role-plays to the class.

1. You are waiting for a plane at the airport. A friendly Japanese woman sitting next to you starts a conversation. She works for an American camera company, perhaps Eastman Kodak, in Japan. You work for a Japanese camera company, perhaps Nikon, in Chicago. Each of you is happy with your work situation and tries to convince the other person that your company has the best management system.

2. You are interviewing for a management job with an American company. The interviewer seems open to innovative ideas, but there has been an adversary relationship between workers and management in the company for many years. Without losing your chances of getting the job, you try to convince the interviewer that this situation must change. The interviewer, who would like to hire you because of your innovative ideas, tries to convince you that the company doesn't really need to change so much.

3. You love to ski and try to go to the mountains on the weekends as often as possible. Therefore, you support the idea of a four-day, ten-hour work week. A fellow employee, on the other hand, likes to play tennis every afternoon after work and wants to continue working five days a week for eight hours a day. The matter will be voted on by the employees tomorrow. Try to persuade the other employee to vote for the four-day work week.

Exercise 3 There is a cynical saying: "Everyone has a price." This means that if someone initially does not want to do something, his or her services can be "bought" if he or she is presented with the right enticement. Just for fun, try the following activity.

Ask another student in the class (or your instructor, if you wish) to do something unusual or something that would very likely elicit a *no* response. For example:

Will you pay for my trip to Paris next week?
Will you marry my brother tomorrow?
Will you do my homework for me?

When the student responds (see p. 23 for ways to say *no*), do not take *no* for an answer. Try to persuade your classmate by presenting various positive or negative consequences. For example:

Well, would you pay for my trip if I gave you a 1 percent interest in my company?

If you don't marry my brother, he will be heartbroken.

If your classmate still refuses to do what you've asked, you must continue to present consequences that are more and more positive or negative until your classmate finally gives in. For example:

If you don't pay for my trip, I will probably lose my entire business because I can't get to Paris to negotiate a big contract.

If you marry my brother, you will be married to the richest, kindest, and most handsome man in my country. He will be devoted to you all your life.

Then change roles so that your partner is now making a request of you. If you work in small groups, let other students in on the laughter this activity produces by sharing a few of your group's conversations with the rest of the class.

109

CHAPTER 8
ETHICAL QUESTIONS

Ethics is a branch of philosophy that concerns human values and conduct, what humans ought to do. *Ought* in this case means what is right and good for people to do.

Today there are two main philosophical schools of thought on what is right and good for people to do. The first says that one should act in a way that brings the greatest pleasure to oneself and to society as a whole. The second says that one should act so that one's actions serve as a model for others. This second theory is a variation of the Golden Rule: "Do unto others as you would have them do unto you." Both of these schools of thought will be considered in this chapter's lecture on the ethical questions involved when people donate, buy, or sell body parts to be transplanted into another person.

Lecture: Organ Transplants: Ethical Issues
Skill A: Cohesion and Reference
Skill B: Keeping the Floor and Taking the Floor

PART ONE

DISCUSSION

Ethics touches every part of our lives. Ethical people make choices based on principle instead of personal advantage. A person who lives according to principles is truly an individual, rather than a member of a "herd." As a class, briefly discuss the following:

1. Consider the choices the following men and women had to make for the sake of principle. In similar circumstances, would you have made the same or similar choices?

   a. Buddha left his family and gave up all his worldly possessions; he vowed to sit in meditation until he achieved enlightenment for the sake of all human beings.
   b. Socrates chose to accept his unjust punishment of drinking poison rather than escape from prison and live in hiding.
   c. Harry Truman chose to drop the atomic bomb and face worldwide criticism because he thought that even more people would die if World War II continued.
   d. Joan of Arc chose to be burned to death rather than deny her belief that her actions were directly guided by God.

2. Choose someone you know who had to face a difficult ethical choice and describe it to the class. It may be a famous person

from your native country, a friend, an acquaintance, or someone you have heard about.

3. What principles do you live by? How did you develop them? Do you ever go against any of them?

   Examples of principles:

   a. Do unto others as you would have them do unto you.
   b. Never lie.
   c. Honor your father and mother.
   d. Never kill.
   e. Never steal.

4. What would you sacrifice to maintain your principles?

5. How should scarce medical resources such as doctors, nurses, hospital beds, expensive drugs, and highly advanced medical machines be distributed to those who need them? In your opinion, should they be given to the most needy or to those who can afford them? If too many people need one item, should the person who will receive it be chosen by lottery, by judges, or by some other method?

FOR SALE: 1 kidney to highest bidder. Call 555–9981. Ask for Harry Highliver.

Out of work family man wants to sell 1 cornea for $50,000 minimum. Write to Box 791 and make offer.

Potential suicide victim wants to leave large inheritance to children. Selling heart, liver, and corneas for $1 million. Call 555-1623 and leave name and phone number on message machine.

VOCABULARY

One way to determine the meaning of a word you haven't heard before is to break it down into root and affixes. If you know the meaning of the root and the meaning of the neighboring affixes (prefixes and suffixes), you can guess what the word means. For example, consider the words *decision, excision,* and *incision:*

de-	= away from	*in-*	= in
ex-	= out	*-cision*	= cut

Therefore, *incision* means "a cut in," *excision* means "a cut out" or "removal," and *decision* means "a cut away from" or "a choice."

In the following exercise, discover the meaning of the words by looking at the meanings of the individual syllables. As a class, write the meaning of each syllable in the blank and then decide what the word means. Some of the blanks have been filled in to provide hints. Consult a dictionary for help.

Example: *trans-* = *across*

plant = to place permanently

-able = able

transplantable = *can be taken across (from one place to another) and placed permanently*

1. *a(d)-* = to

   loc(are) = place

   -at(e) makes the word a verb

   -ion makes the word a noun

   allocation = *distributing (as a share of for a purpose* *giving, putting on one side*

2. *commod(us)* = convenient or useful

   -ity makes the word a noun

   commodity = *useful thing, esp. an article of trade*

3. *com-* = with

   pati = to feel, sympathize

   -ible makes the word *an adjective*

   compatible = *able to exist together; in accord with*

4. *de-* = from

   gener = *yield, create*

   -ative makes the word an adjective *(physical, moral or mental)*

   degenerative = *having lost qualities that are considered normal and desirable*

5. *discrimin (discremen)* = distinction

   -ate makes the noun a *verb*

   to discriminate = *be, make, see, a difference between*

   (against) treat differently; make distinction

6. *humàne* = *tender, kindhearted* *adj*

   -ness makes the word a *noun*

   humaneness = *quality of being humane. human nature*

7. *immuno-* = exempt from service; not vulnerable

   su(b) = _lower in rank_

   press = _force to do sth._

   -ion makes the word a _noun_

   immunosuppression = _safety, security (from disease) exemption (from taxation)_

il –
im –
ir -

8. *in-* = _.... not_

   cur(e) = _bring (a person) back to health._

   -able makes the word a _adjective_

   incurable = _that cannot be cured (incurable diseases)_

9. *ir-* = not

   re- = _again_

   verse = to turn

   -ible = _(able) that can be; fit to be_

   irreversible = _that cannot be reversed or revoked._

10. *pro-* = before

    gnosis = knowing

    prognòsis = _forecast of the probable course of a disease or illness_   _病状之預断._

11. *recipi(ens)* = past participle of *to receive*

    -ent makes the word a noun

    recipient = _person who receives sth._

PART TWO

SKILL A: COHESION AND REFERENCE

By this point in your English studies, you have been exposed to a variety of rules about the English language. Many of these rules are important for clearly connecting ideas and preventing misunderstanding on the part of the listener or reader. Spoken or written language that follows these rules is said to be cohesive; that is, it holds together. Cohesion is what makes a series of sentences into a paragraph and a series of paragraphs into an entire text.

Likewise, it makes a series of sentences into a conversation or a lecture. Cohesion occurs when the meaning in one part of the discourse depends on or explains the meaning in another part. In other words, a unified whole of meaning arises from what would otherwise be just a collection of parts.

How is cohesion maintained? There are various devices used to string together the elements of language to create meaning. One of these devices is called *reference*. Reference is the use of pronouns and other words to refer to a noun that has already been mentioned and is understood. Consider the following sentences, for example:

1. The doctor had to make a choice.
2. The doctor had to decide which of the accident victims to treat first.

These sentences are independent. They seem to be related to the same topic, but the meaning of one sentence does not depend on the meaning of the other. If you create a dependent relationship between two sentences, you connect them so that together they have meaning, although one sentence, alone is ambiguous. For example:

3. The doctor decided to treat the little boy first.
4. He hoped that he had made the right choice.

Sentence 3 establishes that we are talking about the doctor. In Sentence 4, *he* clearly refers to the doctor, but this reference would not be clear without Sentence 3.

Every language has certain words that make reference to other words and therefore depend on those other words for their interpretation. In English, these reference words include personal pronouns, adverbs of time and place, and demonstratives. Personal pronouns include:

Subject and Object Pronouns	Possessive Pronouns	Possessive Adjectives
I, me	mine	my
you	yours	your
we, us	ours	our
he, him	his	his
she, her	hers	her
they, them	theirs	their
it	its (rarely used)	its
one		one's

Two of these words may pose some comprehension problems for you. One is *you* when it is used instead of *one*. Some years ago it was common to say, for example, "One never knows, does one?"

but today it is more common to say, "You never know, do you?" When *you* is used in this way (to refer to people in general rather than to one specific person), it is sometimes difficult to comprehend the referent—who is being referred to.

The other tricky word is *it* used to refer to an idea or concept expressed by a phrase, a whole sentence, a paragraph, or perhaps an entire conversation. For example:

5. The doctor cleaned up the wounds on the little boy's face, ordered some X rays of his head, and told the nurses to get the operating room ready while the medical assistant checked the rest of the boy's body for other injuries.

6. So far, it was going well.

In Sentence 6, the word *it* refers to the treatment described by all of Sentence 5 and perhaps even to the ethical choice the doctor had to make described in Sentences 1 through 4.

Adverbs of time and place are also used to avoid repetition and to "locate" the referent—the person or thing referred to—in space and time. The most common are:

	Near	**Far**
Place	here	there
Time	now	then

Demonstrative pronouns are also used to avoid repetition:

	Near	**Far**
Singular	this	that
Plural	these	those

Comprehension of the exact referent can be difficult when the reference word is used to describe something that cannot be named in one or two words. Consider the following sentences:

7. The surgery was taking a long time; the doctor felt tired, hungry, and worried about the other accident victims who still needed to be treated.

8. That was the way it went some days in the emergency room.

Notice that the word *that* in Sentence 8 refers to the particular circumstance described and feeling conveyed by Sentence 7. And *it* refers to daily life in general. When the demonstrative word comes before rather than after what is being referred to, determining the referent can also be tricky. For example:

9. This was going to be hard.

10. He never enjoyed making life-or-death decisions.

In this case the word *this* in Sentence 9 does not refer to something already mentioned. *This* refers to "making life-or-death decisions" mentioned in the next sentence, Sentence 10.

Although reference words allow you to avoid repetition, they can be ambiguous and confusing if not properly used. Consider the following.

11. The little boy smiled at the doctor as he opened his eyes.

Whose eyes are they? Most likely they are the little boy's eyes. But what if the sentence just before Sentence 10 had been this:

12. In the recovery room, the weary doctor closed his eyes for a moment.

In this case, the reference in Sentence 11 would not be as clear. We could not be certain whose eyes opened, the doctor's or the little boy's. In general, this kind of ambiguity can be avoided by taking care not to overuse reference words and by keeping in mind that there are times when exactly who or what you are talking about must be restated.

As a listener, how can you avoid confusion over what a reference word refers to? One way is to listen actively. When you hear a reference word, ask yourself: Who? Whose? What? When? or Where? For example, when you hear a word such as *there*, you should immediately ask yourself *Where?* and connect the reference word *there* with the place it refers to. Or, to take another example, when you hear the word *it*, you should immediately ask yourself *What?* In this way, you can connect the reference word with its referent quickly without losing track of what the speaker is saying. If you do become confused about a reference word during a lecture, you can indicate this with a question mark in the margin of your notes and ask the instructor or a classmate the appropriate question as soon as you have the opportunity to interrupt politely.

Listen In

Exercise 1 Listen to the lecture once or twice all the way through. Then listen again, and this time focus on the pronouns, adverbs of time and place, and demonstratives. Ask yourself Who? Whose? What? When? or Where? each time you hear one of these words. When you answer these questions, remember that the referent may be heard either before or after the reference word. To guide your listening, certain reference words have been selected from the lecture and listed here. Questions are provided in Items 1 through 5, and the reference words are italicized in Items 1 through 10. For the rest of the items, find the reference word, write the appropriate question, and answer it.

Bone marrow transplant recipient Stesan Morsh and donor Terrence Bailey.

Example: Try to imagine this situation.

Question: What situation?

Answer: The entire story about David needing a transplant and finally getting one.

1. *They* have been told that David's only hope is a liver transplant.

Question: Who has been told?

Answer: _____

2. *This* boy's parents hope that their son's liver can help.

Question: Which boy's parents?

Answer: _____

Heart transplant recipient and his wife examine a heart model.

3. Patients needing organs vastly outnumber donors, *those* who can give organs.

Question: Those what?

Answer: _____

4. Because of *this*, each year thousands of people who could be saved by a routine transplant die.

Question: Because of what?

Answer: _____

5. Are you having trouble clarifying your position on these questions? Well, let's put *it this* way.

Since we do not yet have the means to keep organs alive outside the human body for long periods of time, organs often must be rapidly delivered to needy recipients.

Question: Put what this way?

Answer: _____

Question: Put it what way?

Answer: _____

6. As the sea becomes rougher, *it* is clear to all of you in the boat. . . .

   Question: _____

   Answer: _____

7. Do you trust *his* fairness in making the decision?

   Question: _____

   Answer: _____

8. In *that* case, the only fair method of decision would be some sort of lottery.

   Question: _____

   Answer: _____

9. In other situations so dramatically affecting the public welfare, the government *here* has always intervened.

   Question: _____

   Answer: _____

10. Recently, laws have been proposed that would make *this* a crime.

    Question: _____

    Answer: _____

11. These laws would place the allocation of this precious commodity entirely in the hands of the federal government.

    Question: _____

    Answer: _____

    Question: _____

    Answer: _____

12. I suppose this would be something like harvesting the dead.

    Question: _____

    Answer: _____

13. Some psychologists believe this might present a greater psychological threat to humanity.

Question: _____

Answer: _____

14. The response to that argument has often been that few people, if any, have the wisdom to see what the social good is now.

Question: _____

Answer: _____

15. Nor can they see what it will be in the future.

Question: _____

Answer: _____

Question: _____

Answer: _____

16. The problems with this position seem great, however, because of the shortage of organs and the large number of needy people.

Question: _____

Answer: _____

17. What if three people are in immediate danger of dying from kidney failure, but there is only one kidney? Then this solution does not help.

Question: _____

Answer: _____

18. They would know that no one discriminated against them for any reason.

Question: _____

Answer: _____

19. It becomes even more complex when we realize that certain of these choices, once made, mean that one person will live and others will probably die.

Question: _____

Answer: _____

Exercise 2 Listen to the lecture again. As you listen, make a list of as many of the reference words as you can and who or what each refers to (the referent).

_____

_____

Combine your list with your classmates' lists. How many reference words do you have as a class? As a class, make sure the referents on the list are correct. Are most of the referents people? Ideas?

Speak Out

Exercise 1   Find a brief article in a magazine or newspaper that deals with some type of ethical choice and bring it to class. In small groups, take turns reading your articles aloud. Whenever those who are listening hear a reference word, they should call out the appropriate question. Several people may call out similar questions at the same time. Someone in the group who did not ask the question should answer it. Then the reader of the article should continue.

Exercise 2   Listen to people on t.v. or the radio and to friends and other people you speak with and try to pick out: (1) any examples of ambiguous reference and (2) any examples of extended reference in which the referent is expressed by a whole sentence, paragraph, or conversation, not just one word. Write down these examples so that you can bring them to class and discuss them with your classmates. Consider the following questions:

1. How or why was the reference ambiguous?
2. How could the ambiguity be avoided?
3. What happened because of the ambiguity? For example, was it funny? Was there a misunderstanding?
4. Were the examples of extended reference hard to find? Why or why not?
5. How would you characterize the referents in cases of extended reference? For example, did they tend to be things, people, or ideas?

SKILL B: KEEPING THE FLOOR
AND TAKING THE FLOOR

In conversation, people take turns listening and speaking. Smooth "turn taking" is a critical part of any conversation. The rules that govern turn taking differ in different societies and ethnic groups, since turn taking is in many ways culturally determined. So it is essential to learn how to take your turn according to the rules of the culture whose language you are speaking.

Even among native speakers of the same language, turn taking does not always occur smoothly. For instance, there are many times when what you have to say may be ignored unless you assert your right to say it. Furthermore, people often interpret silence as agreement. In addition, they may assume that you have nothing to say if you do not claim a right to speak. Asserting yourself and speaking out is called "taking the floor." Similarly, if someone interrupts you when you are speaking, you may not want to relinquish your turn at that moment. Refusing to give up a turn is called "keeping the floor."

During a lecture in class, there are appropriate and inappropriate times to take the floor. Unless the instructor specifically tells you to save questions until the end, you are generally free to interrupt in order to:

1. ask for clarification or repetition of a specific point
2. add pertinent information
3. challenge a point

In all three of these instances, you should stick to the immediate topic. Do not raise issues from previous lectures or other sources unless they are particularly relevant; otherwise you risk interrupting the instructor's train of thought and annoying your classmates.

As with all conversational functions in English, there are both polite and impolite ways to "keep the floor" and "take the floor" and rules about when you should be more polite and when you can be less polite. Following are some verbal expressions and nonverbal cues to use to indicate your desire to keep the floor:

Polite

Can (May) I please just get through/say this?
I don't want to lose my train of thought.
Just a minute (second), please.
Let me just finish what I was saying (before I forget).
Let me just say this (one more thing).
Let me just tell you . . .
Please don't interrupt. (in a polite tone)

Impolite

Don't interrupt me!
Let me handle this!
(Shut up and) Let me finish!

**Nonverbal Cues (Polite Depending on the Situation,
Relative Status of Speaker and Listener, etc.)**

signal "stop" with hand
talk louder
talk faster, keeping pauses to a minimum
any combination of the other three

Nonverbal Cues (Impolite)

a threatening gesture
derisive laughter

Here are some expressions for taking the floor:

Polite

Can I just say (add) something here?
Excuse me for interrupting, but . . .
May (Can) I interrupt?
If I could interrupt . . .
If I could just come in here . . .
That's true, but . . .
Yes, but . . .

Impolite, Except among Close Friends

No, you're wrong! (or any derogatory or derisive comment about
the speaker's point of view, followed by your own point of
view)

That's ridiculous!

What a stupid idea!

**Nonverbal Cues (Polite Depending on the Situation,
Relative Status of Speaker and Listener, etc.)**

move closer to the person talking
take an audible breath
put a hand out
raise an index finger

Nonverbal Cues (Always Impolite)

any threatening gesture
derisive laughter

Listen to the following conversations, in which people keep and
take the floor. As you listen, imagine which nonverbal cues you
think they might be giving.

Conversation 1

Erik: I hear they're doing great things now in the field of genetic engineering.

Sylvia: Well, our biology professor spoke to us today about how experimenting with genes can be dangerous. He said . . .

Erik: That's true, but . . .

Sylvia: Let me just tell you the main point he made. He said that newly created genes could accidentally enter the gene pool and cause unimaginable . . .

Erik: Yes, but . . .

Sylvia: Let me just finish what I was saying. These new genes could cause unimaginable genetic changes in the world. And what if these changes were worse than the problems the new genes were developed to correct?

Erik: Yeah, I see what you mean. I hadn't thought of that.

Conversation 2

T.A.:   Well, to continue with some examples of issues that fall into the area of ethics, I'd like to talk about some of the problems with euthanasia.

Sally: (giggling) Oh, are the youth in Asia having problems these days?

T.A.:   That's very clever—now where was I? Oh, yes, the issue of choosing to die instead of living in pain and suffering because of serious disease or aging. The first problem seems to be whether we ever have the right to take another life or not. The law, in fact, says that we certainly do not.

Gina: If I could interrupt, I believe some states allow for extenuating circumstances, and it may not always be such a black-and-white issue.

T.A.:   Oh, I wasn't aware of that. Perhaps you could find out for us exactly what the laws in those states say regarding extenuating circumstances. It would be quite interesting to see how various governmental bodies deal with an ethical issue such as this.

Fred: Excuse me for interrupting, but I already have that information because of the research I did for a term paper I wrote on a similar topic for another class. I could bring it in next time, if you like.

T.A.:   Sure, that would save us quite a bit of time. Thank you.

Listen In

Listen to the lecture once or twice through. Then listen again, this time noting times when you think it would be appropriate to interrupt. Choose at least six points in the lecture where you might interrupt to:

1. ask for clarification or repetition of a specific point
2. add pertinent information
3. challenge a point

Write the gist or main idea of what you would say when you interrupt and indicate which verbal and nonverbal cues you would use to initiate the interruption. Use each of the purposes for interruption above at least once.

_____

_____

_____

_____

_____

_____

_____

_____

Compare your responses with your classmates'. Did you tend to choose the same places in the lecture to interrupt or different places? What were the types of interruptions?

Speak Out

Ethical questions are controversial by definition. Whenever you bring up a question concerning what people ought to do or when you try to sort out what is right and wrong, there is always a variety of opinions. In this activity, you will have a chance to "stand on a soapbox" and give a two-to-three-minute "spiel" (talk) on what you think people ought to do in regard to a particular ethical issue (see the following list of suggestions). Of course, to speak continuously for two to three minutes, you will have to take some time to organize your thoughts before you begin.

Give your spiel in small groups. When you are listening, it will be your task to interrupt the speaker as many times as possible. Since this is only a game, you may play the role of a rude person if you wish, but no more than one or two people in the group should do this to any speaker. When you are the speaker, it will be your task to keep the floor as much as possible. You may want to allow someone to take the floor who has pertinent questions or information, but you should not allow anyone who is being rude to take the floor. During this activity, practice using a variety of verbal and nonverbal cues for keeping and taking the floor. Here are some possible topics, but choose your own if you prefer.

1. using live animals for research
2. declaring someone officially dead when the brain stops rather than when the heart stops
3. buying and selling organs
4. pleading insanity for murder
5. euthanasia
6. appropriate versus inappropriate uses of technology (e.g., nuclear fission)
7. genetic engineering (e.g., changing existing organisms or developing entirely new ones)
8. shortening sentences of prison inmates for participating in potentially dangerous medical research
9. respecting the wishes of the dead (wills, informal requests)
10. birth control
11. inappropriate punishments for crimes such as drunk driving
12. placing the elderly in nursing homes

CHAPTER 9
THE ARTS

Music is a universal art form. Every culture has developed some type of music. The rhythms, sounds, and lyrics of music can have a profound effect on human thought and can stir up the deepest emotions. We know that since the beginning of recorded time (and we suspect even earlier) people have enjoyed music. While we still enjoy the music of the past, one of today's most popular forms of music—rock and roll—actually began quite recently. In the lecture in this chapter, you will hear more about the beginnings of rock and roll and its development over the past thirty-five years.

Lecture: The Changing Sounds of Rock and Roll
Skill A: Distinguishing between Fact and Opinion
Skill B: Expressing Disbelief and Doubt

PART ONE

DISCUSSION

As a class or in small groups, discuss the following:

1. What kinds of music are most popular in your native country?
2. What kinds of music are most popular among your friends?
3. How often do you listen to music at home?
4. Have you attended a live concert? If so, describe one you have enjoyed.
5. What are your favorite types of music and who are your favorite musical performers?
6. Do you like rock and roll? Why or why not?
7. Do you play any musical instruments? If so, describe what type of music you like to play and why. If not, have you considered learning to play an instrument? Why would you like to play this particular instrument?

VOCABULARY

The following list of words has been taken from the lecture in this chapter. Fill in the crossword puzzle with the correct forms of the words on the list. See p. 187 for the answers.

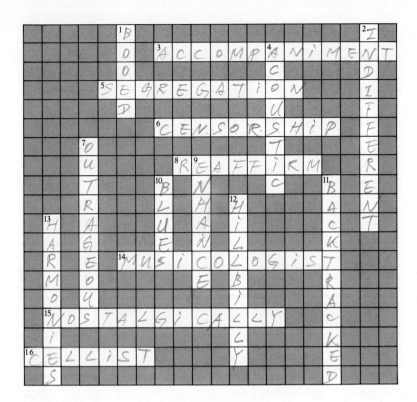

Rock and Roll Crossword Puzzle

accompaniment
acoustic 听觉的
to backtrack
blues
to boo （喝倒彩）
cellist 大提琴奏者
censorship
to enchance ? enhance
harmonies
hillbilly 山地居民(贫农)
indifferent
musicologist
nostalgically 怀旧,怀念
outrageous
to reaffirm
segregation 分离

Across Clues

3. music that is played while the principal singer sings
5. the separation of one group from another based on race, class, or ethnic origin
6. the removal of offensive material from communications
8. restate with confidence
14. one who studies music from a historical and scientific standpoint
15. in a manner that shows longing for something out of the past
16. one who plays the cello, the next-to-largest member of the violin family

Down Clues

1. shouted disapproval or contempt
2. having no preference; not interested in anything
4. of or relating to sound; natural sound, not electronic
7. extremely unusual; fantastic
9. make more valuable, beautiful, desirable; upgrade
10. a style of music characterized by sadness
11. moved backwards; backed up
12. a person from a mountainous backwoods area
13. pleasant or congruent arrangements of parts, such as musical chords 一致的，调和的

PART TWO

SKILL A: DISTINGUISHING BETWEEN FACT AND OPINION

Suppose you are looking for a good investment. You have heard that old records sometimes skyrocket in value, so you decide to go to a record trade show. At the show, many interesting offers appear, but you are most interested in the old Beatles recording of "She Loves You" performed without drummer Ringo Starr. Apparently, this is an unusual, one-of-a-kind recording, and the salesperson offers it for $890. In the salesperson's opinion, the recording will triple in value within the next few weeks and if you are smart, you will buy it now and resell it when the value goes up. How can you determine if this is indeed a terrific deal or if it is just the salesperson's opinion?

You would gather information from other experts at the show, wouldn't you? Careful research would help you find facts. Of course, you don't separate fact from òpinion only when making investments. In most other situations, conversations, and certainly in lectures, you try to distinguish between fact and opinion. Facts are based on direct evidence and can be proved through experience or observation. However, facts can be "slippery." They can change with time. It may be a fact that a record is a terrific bargain today, but what if records become obsolete tomorrow and everyone buys tapes and discs? Then the record may be worthless. Furthermore, statements that seem to be based on solid evidence may be inaccurate. For example, "Elvis Presley was the first rock and roll singer" is a false statement. Facts *must* be checked for accuracy.

An opinion is defined as someone's feeling, belief, or judgment about someone or something. It is not objective; personal biases and attitudes influence opinions. In the lecture in this chapter, many personal opinions are given. How can you distinguish these opinions from facts?

First, look for words that signal that the statement may be an opinion. Words like *probably, most likely, usually, often, sometimes,* and *on occasion* limit a statement of fact and indicate the possibility of other opinions. Other obvious opinion words include:

in my opinion	I feel
it seems to me	personally
I believe	personally speaking
I think	

Second, look for adjectives that may express value judgments such as *pretty, ugly, safe, dangerous, good, bad, extraordinary,* and *outrageous.* Usually words such as these indicate an opinion rather than a fact. Third, question the expertise of the speakers. Should you believe them? Are they reliable sources? For example, are they well-known and respected authorities in their fields, or are they merely popularizers of current fads? Fourth, question the authorities that speakers use as their sources. Are these people reliable experts? Finally, try to formulate a contrasting point of view. Is this view as reasonable and as acceptable as the speaker's? If so, what the speaker is presenting may be opinion and not fact.

Listen In

Listen to the lecture at least twice through. Then look over the following statements and listen once more. This time, your instructor will stop the tape periodically. The first time the tape is stopped, answer Item 1; the second time the tape is stopped, answer Item 2; and so on. For each item, first decide whether you think the statement is a fact or an opinion and explain why. If you decide a statement is an opinion, indicate whether you agree or disagree with this opinion and explain why. Two examples have been provided.

Elvis Presley in concert, Tampa, Florida, 1956.

Bill Haley and the Comets.

133

Examples: Music is a universal phe-nomenon.

<u>X</u> Fact _____ Opinion

Why? *Because musicologists are probably reliable sources.*

_____ Agree _____ Disagree

Why? _____

_____

_____

_____

Music has the most meaning in the cultural context in which it is created.

_____ Fact <u>X</u> Opinion

Why? *Because speaker said "I think" and "it seems to me."*

_____

<u>X</u> Agree _____ Disagree

Why? *Personal experience; I don't fully understand music from other countries.*

1. The name *rock and roll* comes from Alan Freed.

_____ Fact _____ Opinion

Why? _____

_____

_____

_____

_____ Agree _____ Disagree

Why? _____

_____

_____

_____

2. The blues are part of the black musical tradition in America.

_____ Fact _____ Opinion

Why? _____

_____

_____

_____

_____ Agree _____ Disagree

Why? _____

_____

_____

_____

3. The actual beginning of rock and roll music was on April 12, 1954, in New York City when Bill Haley and the Comets recorded "Rock Around the Clock."

_____ Fact _____ Opinion

Why? _____

_____

_____

_____

_____ Agree _____ Disagree

Why? _____

_____

_____

_____

4. Rockabilly is a mixture of the blues harmonies of black music and the hillbilly sounds of white music.

_____ Fact _____ Opinion

Why? _____

_____

_____

_____

_____ Agree _____ Disagree

Why? _____

_____

_____

_____

5. The '50s generation was eager to grow up.

_____ Fact _____ Opinion

Why? _____

_____

_____

_____

_____ Agree _____ Disagree

Why? _____

_____

_____

_____

6. Teenagers in every society have rebelled against or resisted their parents in some way.

_____ Fact _____ Opinion

Why? _____

_____

_____

_____

_____ Agree _____ Disagree

Why? _____

_____

_____

_____

7. In the '60s there was a mood of confusion and instability.

_____ Fact _____ Opinion

Why? _____

_____

_____

_____

_____ Agree _____ Disagree

Why? _____

_____

_____

_____

8. Bob Dylan was more a poet than a songwriter.

_____ Fact _____ Opinion

Why? _____

_____

_____

_____

_____ Agree _____ Disagree

Why? _____

_____

_____

_____

9. At first, concert audiences didn't like Dylan's new sound.

_____ Fact _____ Opinion

Why? _____

_____

_____

_____

_____ Agree _____ Disagree

Why? _____

_____

_____

_____

10. Protest rock condemned the evils of our society.

_____ Fact _____ Opinion

Why? _____

_____

_____

_____

_____ Agree _____ Disagree

Why? _____

_____

_____

_____

11. The Beatles
appeared
respectable to
adults.

_____ Fact _____ Opinion

Why? _____

_____

_____

_____ Agree _____ Disagree

Why? _____

_____

_____

_____

12. The Beatles had a
good sense of
humor.

_____ Fact _____ Opinion

Why? _____

_____

_____

_____ Agree _____ Disagree

Why? _____

_____

_____

_____

13. The Beatles' music
has the most
original sound in
popular music.

_____ Fact _____ Opinion

Why? _____

_____

_____

_____ Agree _____ Disagree

Why? _____

_____

_____

_____

14. The Rolling Stones were outrageous compared with the Beatles.

_____ Fact _____ Opinion

Why? _____

_____

_____

_____

_____ Agree _____ Disagree

Why? _____

_____

_____

_____

15. Soul music is an expression of black pride.

_____ Fact _____ Opinion

Why? _____

_____

_____

_____

_____ Agree _____ Disagree

Why? _____

_____

_____

_____

Speak Out

For this activity, you will be a critic of the arts. First, choose one of the arts that interests you, such as architecture, dance, music, painting, sculpture, or theater. Next, find a visual example of the type of art you've chosen. You might find a postcard with a repro-duction of a painting, a newspaper advertisement for a movie, play, dance performance, or opera, or a picture from a book on architecture. Gather as much factual information as you can about the particular work you've selected by reading the text in the ad or on the back of the postcard or the caption under the photo in the book. For example, who wrote the script, who was the choreographer, where is the building located, what material did the sculptor use?

Then prepare a one- to two-minute critique of the work to present to your classmates. Evaluate the work and decide whether you like it or not and whether you'll give it a favorable review or an unfavorable one. When you present your critical review, include as many facts and opinions from the work as you can in the allotted time. Your classmates will try to remember three facts and three opinions from your presentation. After each presentation, discuss the various facts and opinions the speaker included. Which do you and your classmates usually find most interesting, facts or opinions? Why?

SKILL B: EXPRESSING DISBELIEF AND DOUBT

As discussed in "Skill A," people sometimes present statements as proven facts when actually the facts have not yet been substantiated. Or people may even present statements that are merely opinions as proven facts. At such times, you may want to express doubt or disbelief. The following expressions are used to express doubt or disbelief:

Informal

Don't give me that.
Get out of here!
I doubt it (that).
I'll believe that when I see it!
No way!
(Oh) Come on!
(Oh) Sure!
Really?
That can't be true.

Formal

Are you sure that's (it's) right (correct)?
Are you sure that's (it's) okay?
Could he (she) really do (think) that?
Do you (they) really believe that?

You may wonder why "I don't believe it!", which at first seems an obvious expression of disbelief, is not on the list. This is because "I don't believe it!" is actually an expression normally used to indicate surprise on the part of the speaker rather than disbelief.

If you feel strong disbelief and are eager to have proof that what the speaker says is true, you may add one of the following expressions. These are requests for proof or questions about the speaker's sources.

How do you know that?
Show me.
Where?
Where did you get that information?
Where did you hear that?

Of course, questions like "Where did you get that information?", "How do you know that?" and "Where did you hear that?" can also be genuine requests for information asked out of curiosity.

Whenever you use any of these expressions to indicate doubt or disbelief, be careful not to make the speaker feel that you are calling him or her a liar. Take care to show through your intonation that you trust the person but simply disbelieve what he or she has said.

Listen to the following conversations, which include examples of formal and informal ways to express disbelief, keeping in mind that you will never be considered rude if you speak too formally. It is only by being inappropriately informal that you may be considered ill-mannered when expressing doubt or disbelief. Notice also that sometimes intonation alone can express doubt or disbelief.

Conversation 1

Carl: Professor Johnson, I'd like to talk to you about my art project for my senior thesis.
Professor Johnson: No time like the present, Carl. Have a seat. What would you like to do?
Carl: Are you sure it's okay? I know how busy you are.
Professor Johnson: It's fine.
Carl: Well, I'd like to do something really imaginative and creative, something like my friend Howard did for his master's thesis.
Professor Johnson: What was that?
Carl: He filled the administration building entrance hall with white paper cups, and that was his project.
Professor Johnson: And he got his master's for that?
Carl: Yes, he did.
Professor Johnson: I find that hard to believe. You'll have to think of something else, Carl—another type of project.

Notice that the professor expresses disbelief twice in this conversation, once with intonation when he said, "And he got his master's for that?" and the second time when he used the expression, "I find that hard to believe." In both cases the professor is being polite and would still be considered polite if he were speaking to a peer

adj. + N.

it's a fifty-foot-tall bldg.

the bldg is fifty feet tall

rather than a student. The student expresses doubt by using the expression, "Are you sure it's okay?" He probably has had a hard time getting an appointment and fears he may be interrupting the professor at a busy time.

Conversation 2

Mr. Jones: My twelve-year-old son is in a rock band, and the band is going to make $40,000 in the next three months.
Mr. Smith: I'll believe that when I see it.
Mr. Jones: Yes, really they will. And the most amazing thing is that they have a twelve-year-old manager. She does all the negotiating for the concerts.
Mr. Smith: Oh, sure!
Mr. Jones: Yes—and she's really first-rate. These twelve-year-olds are booked for concerts in Chicago, Detroit, Denver, Miami, Atlanta, and Philadelphia in the next six weeks alone.
Mr. Smith: Yeah, right—and I'm Mick Jagger.

This conversation between two fathers is informal and courteous until the last line when Mr. Smith becomes sarcastic and says, "Yeah, right—and I'm Mick Jagger" to express his strong disbelief.

Conversation 3

Jenny: I'd really love to be a prima ballerina.
Al: Well, then, you'll have to do more than take lessons once a week. Nureyev danced until his feet bled, and he kept on dancing.
Jenny: I find that hard to believe. How do you know that?
Al: I saw it in a movie. He was so dedicated you wouldn't believe it! With bleeding feet he just danced and danced and danced some more. I saw it all in the movie.
Jenny: Could he really do that?
Al: Yes, it was the most incredible thing I've ever seen.

Jenny expresses her disbelief of Al's statements formally, with a gentle, moderate tone, and therefore is polite.

Conversation 4

Professor Starr: Today I'm going to talk about Mozart, the musical genius who performed concerts on the pianoforte for the royalty of Europe at the age of eight.
Rachel: Oh, come on!
Professor Starr: It's true. Not only that, he was already composing music at the age of five.
Rachel: I doubt it.
Professor Starr: Well, why don't you see me after class for my list of references if you'd like to look into the matter further. But for now, we'll concentrate on a discussion of Mozart's music.

Rachel's words and her aggressive tone are rude. Professor Starr, on the other hand, is extraordinarily patient with Rachel.

Listen In

Listen to the lecture again. Whenever you hear a statement that you think might not be a proven fact, stop the tape and jot down the statement and an appropriate expression to express your doubt or disbelief. If you want some suggestions for places to stop the tape, look back at the "Listen In" exercise for "Skill A" and use some of the statements provided there. Then find some more on your own. Be sure to try using a variety of expressions to express your doubt or disbelief.

Soul singer Aretha Franklin.

_____

_____

_____

_____

_____

_____

Mick Jagger and The Rolling Stones.

_____

_____

_____

_____

_____

_____

Speak Out

Exercise 1 For this activity, get ready to "Fool Your Friends." To begin the activity, divide into two teams. Then share with the rest of the people on your team any interesting or unusual facts in your life that have to do with the arts. These events do not have to involve you directly, but you must be connected to them in some way. Here are several examples.

1. One of my drawings is on display in the city hall in my hometown.
2. My father-in-law is a famous actor.
3. I once got a standing ovation for my dancing at a folk-dance festival.
4. When I was seventeen, I won third prize in a whistling contest.
5. My brother is a well-known graffiti artist.

After you've searched your memory thoroughly to come up with real events, take a few minutes to make up some events that never actually happened and share these with your teammates, too.

The next step is to choose which of these real and imaginary biographical "facts" your team wants to use to try to stump or fool the other team. Then take turns presenting these "facts" to the other team. You may choose to say something about yourself, or you may say something about one of your teammates. (If you have trouble keeping a straight face when you are not telling the truth, you might prefer to say something about a classmate instead of yourself.)

After you have presented your "fact," it will be up to a member of the other team to respond with, "Okay, I believe that," or with one of the expressions of doubt or disbelief. If the opposing team member is correct—that is, the response matches the type of statement (factual or made-up)—the opposing team gets a point. If you have managed to stump the opposing team member and he or she either believes you when you are fooling or doubts you when you are telling the truth, your team gets the point.

Exercise 2   Look over the following unfinished conversations. Choose a partner and together complete one or more of them. Use expressions of doubt or disbelief in your conversations. The first one has been completed for you as a sample. If you like, create one or more of your own conversations, using the sample as a model. If time permits, change partners and do the activity again. Finally, with your partner, choose one of the conversations you've devised to present to the rest of the class.

Conversation 1

A: I went to a terrific concert last night.
B: Oh—which one?
A: It was a John Cage concert, and a woman played the cello underwater.
B: No way!
A: Not only that, but the piano player was underwater, too.
B: Get out of here!
A: Really—John Cage concerts are always far out!
B: Yeah, I know, but I'll believe a woman can play a cello underwater when I see it!

Conversation 2

A: Do you remember the contemporary artist named Christo who wrapped the coast of Australia in canvas and an entire island in pink plastic?
B: Yeah, why?
A: Because his latest project is wrapping the Eiffel Tower in blue silk.
B:
A:
B:
Etc.

Conversation 3

A: What a disaster at the theater tonight!
B: Why? What happened?
A: We were trying to rehearse, and first the lights went out, then the scenery fell over, then the leading man was taken to the hospital with food poisoning, and, as if that weren't enough, we put out a fire in the trash can in the restroom just in time! I think someone is trying to keep the play from opening.
B:
A:
B:
Etc.

Conversation 4

A: Did you hear what your friend David did?

B: No, what?

A: He had a waiter come into the auditorium where he and 300 other students were taking their law exams and serve him a three-course lunch.

B:

A:

B:

Etc.

CHAPTER 10
ENERGY AND MATTER

The energy from the sun warms the earth. You can feel that it does this when you walk barefoot on warm grass or across hot sand. The energy from a rushing river can be changed into electrical energy, which can cause washing machines to run and bulbs to light up rooms. These are examples of the relationship between energy and matter that we might experience every day. But what are the laws of nature that govern the relationship between energy and matter? In the present age, we look to the physicists for answers to questions such as this one. In past ages, however, philosophers were often the "priests of science" who proposed the theories about or "discovered" the laws of nature. Some people believe that the laws of nature described in past ages are merely mistakes or superstitions and that the principles proposed by physicists today are final and complete descriptions of nature. But what about the people of the future? What principles will they regard as the laws of nature? The lecture in this chapter discusses these issues.

Lecture: Discovering the Laws of Nature

Skill A: What to Do When You Understand Each Word and Still Don't Understand

Skill B: Giving and Receiving Compliments

PART ONE

DISCUSSION

Divide into small groups so that, if possible, there is at least one person in each group who has had a general science or physics course. Then discuss the following:

1. In what ways did you learn in school about the physical laws or principles that operate in the universe? For example, did you learn about these laws through textbooks, lectures, class discussions, or laboratory experiments?

2. In your everyday life, in what ways have you learned about the physical laws operating in the universe? For example, did you learn about these laws from reading newspapers and magazines, listening to the news or other programs on t.v. or radio, talking with friends, or observing everyday phenomena?

3. What are a few things that you've learned about physical laws that stand out in your mind?

4. Briefly share your understanding of the following concepts:

energy   motion
gravity   space
light   time
matter

5. Select the concept in Question 4 that you best understand. Do you think that your understanding of this concept is more correct than the understanding of a student five years ago? Fifteen years ago? Fifty years ago? Two hundred and fifty years ago? Twenty-five hundred years ago? Why do you feel this way?

6. Herman von Helmholtz (1821–1894), a German physiologist who contributed to the development of the principle of conservation of energy and the theory of electricity, said: "The originator of a new concept . . . finds, as a rule, that it is much more difficult to find out why other people do not understand him than it was to discover the new truths." In what ways do you think this statement is true or not true? Give specific examples if you can.

VOCABULARY

Exercise 1 Many English words have more than one meaning. Sometimes the meanings are quite similar, but often they are very different. The words in the following list are defined as they are used in the lecture. Look over these words and definitions. Then choose the sentences in the following exercise that use the words as they are defined in the vocabulary list.

Example: *matter* that which is material, physical, not mental or spiritual

       a. The matter in that box is coal.
       b. It doesn't matter.
       c. It's only a matter of time.

contemporary person of approximately the same age as another person living at the same time

cosmos the universe considered as an orderly system

relative not absolute, dependent on something else

divine sacred, holy, having the nature of a deity

1. contemporary
       a. I love contemporary painting.
       b. Einstein was a contemporary of Niels Bohr.
       c. Have you read any contemporary books on the subject of energy?

2. cosmos

    a. He likes to read *Cosmos Magazine.*
    b. The cosmos she planted in the garden came up late this year.
    c. He often wondered about the nature of the cosmos.

3. relative

    a. My cousin Pete is my favorite relative.
    b. Time and space are relative to each other.
    c. He finished the exam with relative ease.

4. divine

    a. "You look divine tonight, my dear!" he exclaimed.
    b. Many cultures have places that they regard as divine.
    c. To divine water, you hold a Y-shaped stick and walk around until the end of the stick points suddenly toward the ground.

Exercise 2   Look over the following words and their definitions. Then pick out the sentences in the exercise that use the words correctly.

manifestation   form, aspect

metaphysical   having to do with the branch of philosophy that deals with the nature of truth and knowledge in the universe

such and such   a condition, person, place, thing, or time not specifically mentioned

wild-goose chase   unfruitful attempt

1. manifestation

    a. She met a manifestation at the party.
    b. One manifestation of electrical energy is lightning.
    c. The manifestation he wrote was not acceptable to his contemporaries.

2. metaphysical

    a. He had a metaphysical at the doctor's office.
    b. She metaphysicals on her way back to work.
    c. They were both interested in metaphysical ideas.

3. such and such

    a. The instructor gave this example to illustrate the theory: If you were going at such and such a speed for such and such an amount of time through space, the amount of time that seemed to pass on earth might be quite different.
    b. He was such and such a difficult instructor that the student wondered if he should wait until someone else taught the physics course.
    c. They were not interested in metaphysical ideas such and such as these.

4. wild-goose chase

    a. During the mating season for geese, we often see one wild-goose chase another goose.

    b. The quest for a unified field theory encompassing all the laws of nature may turn out to be a wild-goose chase.

    c. It was their first wild-goose chase, and they were proud of their success.

PART TWO

SKILL A: WHAT TO DO WHEN YOU UNDERSTAND EACH WORD AND STILL DON'T UNDERSTAND

Have you shopped for a computer or an automobile lately? If so, you may have encountered a salesperson whom you seemed to comprehend at first but soon found difficult to follow. Perhaps you thought you comprehended this person at first because you understood each individual word. However, as the salesperson proceeded to describe a particular product, you may have felt that even though you understood each word, you were not following what was being said. This happens to everyone, even native speakers of a language. Anyone who is trying to understand a complex new subject or concept may have a problem with comprehension even when each word used to talk about the subject is familiar. In addition to the complexity of the subject, the length of the sentences and the speaker's rhythm and intonation can sometimes cause confusion.

For example, when you listen to the lecture in this chapter, "Discovering the Laws of Nature," you may find that some of the concepts from the field of physics are difficult to comprehend even though all of the vocabulary words may be familiar to you. The speaker may use exceptionally long sentences that would be a challenge for anyone, or the speaker may pause and hesitate and change the rhythm in a way that confuses you.

What can you do when you find yourself in such a situation? First, don't panic. Everyone gets confused from time to time. If you are having problems understanding, some of your classmates probably are also.

Second, continue to take notes even though they may not be perfect, because you can use these notes later to ask an instructor or one of your classmates to help you. Your notes may consist of only a few scattered nouns and verbs, but they will be useful in helping you determine exactly where you got confused.

Third, continue your effort to concentrate on the topic. When you become confused, it's easy to give up and think about things such as lunch, the upcoming international students' party, or your next class.

Fourth, in order to pick up the thread of what is being said, listen for the nouns and verbs in the next several sentences. These words convey the essence of meaning. For example, consider this sentence: These principles of physics, however they have been expressed by any people in history, reveal the essential harmony of the world and the intelligence that seems to operate within it. If you were not able to follow this sentence when you heard it, but you still jotted down a few nouns and verbs such as *principles*, *expressed*, *reveal*, and *harmony*, you would get the essence of the idea and have some key words to use in asking for help later on. In addition to nouns and verbs, jot down any words that make the sentence negative, such as *never* and *not*. Without these words, you're likely to interpret your notes later to mean the opposite of what the speaker intended.

Fifth, try repeating to yourself a sentence you haven't grasped if there is a natural pause that allows you time to do so. If this does not help, you might try punctuating the sentence differently— that is, changing the rhythm, stress, or intonation patterns as you repeat it to yourself. Sometimes this is all it takes to manage the mysterious leap from muddle to "Aha!", from incomprehension to understanding.

Finally, it's easier to understand a lecture if you familiarize yourself with the topic beforehand. Therefore, complete the assigned readings before the lecture. If there are no assigned readings or if the readings are very difficult, look up some general information on the topic in a handbook or text designed for the course or for a similar course at a lower level.

COSMOGRAPHIE.

Ptolemaic planetary system.

Listen In

Exercise 1   Listen to the lecture once through. Then listen again. Take notes as you listen the second time, keeping in mind the suggestions of things you can do when you seem to understand each word but still don't understand. Which of the suggestions worked best for you? Are there any areas of your notes that are incomplete? If so, use the words you wrote down to formulate a question to ask a classmate or your instructor in order to fill this gap.

Copernican planetary
system.

Exercise 2   Listen to the lecture again, filling in any gaps in your
notes as necessary. Then look over your notes and paraphrase
and/or summarize each of the major ideas to make sure that you
really understand everything you wrote down.

Speak Out

Exercise 1   Earlier in this chapter, the example of the automobile
salesperson or computer salesperson was given to represent
ordinary situations in which you may understand the words
someone uses, but you do not grasp the whole idea. In small
groups, discuss the following:

1. What situations have you been in in which you understood each
    word but missed the point of what someone was saying? What
    did you do? What was the result? Did you devise a strategy you
    could use in the future (for example, asking for repetition or
    restatement, asking the speaker to give you an example or
    analogy, making eye contact with the speaker and raising your
    eyebrows or shrugging your shoulders)?

2. What techniques do instructors use to help you understand? Do
    they, for example, use study guides, charts, diagrams, or
    outlines?

3. What techniques do you use during conversations to present concepts that may be difficult to understand? For example, do you gesture with your hands? Do you draw diagrams?

Exercise 2   As a class or in small groups, take turns describing what happens to energy and matter in the following everyday situations. Most of the vocabulary should be familiar, but the concepts may be a bit tricky. Use the strategies from this section and any others you and your classmates shared during the previous discussion to help you understand the concepts your fellow students explain and express them as clearly as possible when it is your turn to speak. You may want to consult a reference book for help.

1. blowing out a candle
2. riding a bicycle
3. grinding food in the garbage disposal
4. reflecting sunlight with a mirror onto a piece of paper
5. starting a car engine
6. planting a seed in a sunny garden
7. baking a cake
8. slipping on ice
9. rowing a boat
10. shooting an arrow
11. the turning of a windmill
12. the rising tides during a full moon

SKILL B: GIVING AND RECEIVING COMPLIMENTS

"Flattery will get you everywhere," people say. By this they mean that receiving compliments is so pleasant that if you flatter them at the right moment they would probably be willing to do anything you ask—within reason, of course. And sometimes people say, "Flattery will get you nowhere." By this they mean that whatever it is you want, you're not going to talk them into it by using flattery—compliments that they suspect may not be sincere.

You may merely want to give compliments and not receive anything in return except perhaps some form of "thank you." In this case, you must be careful to give the compliments at appropriate times, you must not give too many compliments, and you must take care that the adjectives or analogies you use are not overstatements; otherwise, it might be suspected that you're only giving the compliments because you want something. Clearly, giving compliments can be tricky. The timing, number, and phrasing of the compliments are crucial to how they will be received.

First, let's deal with timing. Compliments will be regarded as sincere when the recipient feels they are deserved. People usually feel compliments are deserved when they've accomplished something, anything from cooking a great dinner to devising a new theory in physics. Compliments are also appreciated when the recipient needs encouragement. For example, a friend might be momentarily discouraged with his or her pronunciation of English. A compliment or two to remind your friend how far he or she has come would be "just what the doctor ordered" to cure these "pronunciation blues." If you wish to compliment someone's appearance or personality, this might also be just the right sort of encouragement at a particular moment. But the timing of this type of compliment must be just right so as not to cause embarrassment for a shy or reserved person, for example.

Second, let's consider the number of compliments. How many compliments can you give at one time without overdoing it? This can vary from situation to situation, but a good rule of thumb for most situations is:

One's okay,
Two are fine,
But stop at three and draw the line.

One important exception is the number of compliments you can give at one time to a superior or someone in a position of authority. In this case, one compliment is the limit. More than this and you may risk sounding as if you are insincere and only flattering this person.

Third, there are innumerable ways to phrase compliments. Frequently, the main elements in compliments are adjectives and analogies. Words such as *terrific, great, wonderful, fantastic, neat, marvelous,* or any current slang word synonymous with one of these are commonly used. These words are perfectly acceptable, but if you're feeling a bit more imaginative you may prefer to use other adjectives or to formulate analogies. For example, consider this compliment given by a friend to a young scientist:

Hank, you're really a special person. You have a heart as big as the ocean. Even though you're working hard on developing that theory, you still made time to raise money for the hospital.

Finally, when you give a compliment, you may want to introduce it with one of the following expressions:

Just between you and me . . .
I don't mind saying (telling you) . . .

I'd like to compliment you on . . .

If you ask me . . .

I've been meaning to tell you . . .

When you receive a compliment, a simple "thank you" is an appropriate and gracious response. If you want to express your feelings more fully, you may use one of the following expressions:

Coming from you, that's a real compliment (that means a lot).

Do you really think so? How nice (sweet, kind) of you to say that.

I appreciate your saying that.

I'm really glad (pleased) you think so (feel that way).

I'm very flattered.

That (your opinion) means a lot to me.

That's nice to hear.

That's very kind (nice, sweet) of you. ⁄

Thanks, I needed that!

You've made my day!

What a nice (lovely, sweet) thing to say!

To show modesty:

Oh! I can't take all the credit for that.

When you receive a compliment, you may not feel deserving of it, or you may want to express humility by denying that the compliment is true. This is perfectly all right, but don't protest more than once or twice before you give in and accept the compliment graciously. Otherwise you might seem to be saying that the compliment is worthless and not appreciated. Or people might think you are "protesting too much" and really looking for even *more* compliments.

Sometimes you may receive a compliment that you feel is inappropriate. If so, the polite and gracious response is still "thank you." Generally, no further response is given for an inappropriate compliment, because some people consider it bad manners to correct someone. But you may choose to do so with friends when the situation is very informal.

Listen to the following conversations, which provide examples of appropriate and inappropriate ways to give and receive compliments. First listen to these conversations between an instructor and his students.

Conversation 1: In the hall, after class.

Ron: Mr. McGovern, you are such a very good teacher. I like your class so much. I'm learning so much. I like you so-o-o much.
Mr. McGovern: Oh, uh . . . thank you, Ron. Well, I'm on my way to an appointment right now.

Ron's compliments were inappropriate. His comments were too general, too intimate, too repetitive, too many, and given at an inappropriate time.

Conversation 2: In the professor's office, during office hours.

Sandra: Oh, Mr. McGovern, that was a great class. I never understood the second law of thermodynamics before, and now I feel like I could explain to anyone else who doesn't understand it.
Mr. McGovern: Thank you, Sandra. I appreciate your saying that.

Sandra's compliment was appropriate because she praised a specific accomplishment, kept her statements brief, and timed her compliment appropriately.

Now listen to this conversation between several senior citizens.

Conversation 3

Martin: Larry! Helen! Hello! Who's winning?
Helen: Oh, hello, Martin.
Larry: Hi, Martin. Not me! I can never seem to beat Helen at checkers. Just between you and me, she's definitely the checker champion around here.
Helen: Oh, I wouldn't say that. I just win a few games now and then.
Martin: Oh, no, Helen, Larry's right. You're definitely the best player here.
Helen: Well, thank you both very much.
Larry: Hey, Martin, you were looking pretty good last night at the party. I couldn't believe how well you danced! I didn't know you knew how to do all that.
Martin: (chuckling) I don't! It was my first time—my daughter pulled me out onto the dance floor and I had to do it. But I wasn't really any good. In fact, I was terrible. You know that law of nature that says, "You just can't teach an old dog new tricks"!
Helen: Come on, Marty. That's not a law of nature! This is the generation dedicated to the principle of lifelong learning! And I don't mind telling you that you looked just fine out on the dance floor. And what's more, your daughter looked simply beautiful!
Martin: Well, thanks. Coming from you, that means a lot. You're quite a dancer yourself.

Helen: (laughing) Oh, I can't take all the credit. My partner helped some.

Larry: Oh, no—I hardly did anything. Helen really is a wonderful dancer. She's so graceful and light on her feet. She should give lessons. Better yet, she should go on stage in New York or be in the movies. She's as good as any of the dancers you see there.

Helen: Now Larry, flattery will get you nowhere today. You're losing this game of checkers, and I'm not going to let you win no matter how many compliments you give me.

Martin: That's telling him, Helen!

Later in the day these three friends meet again.

Conversation 4

Larry: Martin, what's wrong? You look a bit worried.

Martin: Well, I'm not worried exactly, but I am confused and feeling very old. I wish I had Helen's attitude about the principle of lifelong learning. You always seem so in touch with current ideas, Helen.

Helen: I appreciate your saying that, but what brought all this on?

Martin: Well, I was trying to help my grandson with his physics homework, and I'm afraid I wasn't much help at all. I don't really understand some of the new theories.

Larry: Well, if you ask me, Martin, you were wonderful to even try to help him. A lot of grandfathers wouldn't take the time.

Martin: Thanks, I needed that. But I still wish I knew more about what's happening in the field of physics these days.

Larry: Why is that so important to you?

Martin: It seems to me that young people today have a different view of the world than we did when we were young, and I'd like to understand it.

Helen: Well, that's admirable, Martin. Sounds to me like you *are* interested in lifelong learning after all. In fact, I've been meaning to tell you that you're one of the brightest, most stimulating, most adventuresome and forward-thinking men I know.

Martin: Why, thanks, Helen! That kind of flattery will get you everywhere!

Listen In

Exercise 1 Listen to a t.v. soap opera or situation comedy. Each time you hear a compliment, jot it down. Listen until you hear at least three compliments. Describe the situations and report the compliments you heard to the class.

_____

_____

_____

_____

_____

_____

Exercise 2 Listen to the conversations from "Skill B" again. Note how the speakers give and receive compliments in the senior citizens' conversations. Were there any compliments that you felt were not appropriate? Why or why not?

Speak Out

Exercise 1 In groups of three to five, imagine that you are a team of scientists living in the year 2200. You have recently made some important discoveries about the relationship of energy and matter. It is now your task to put these theories to practical use by designing a device that converts energy into matter. As your scientific team tackles this task and brainstorms various ideas, there should be opportunities to compliment your teammates on their ideas and to receive a few compliments yourself. Make whatever drawings or diagrams you need for illustrating your ideas as you go along. As a group, make a drawing or diagram that illustrates the device your team develops.

Exercise 2 Now imagine that your research team is going to an international conference. Present your device to the other "scientists" (your classmates) assembled in the main conference hall. Use

159

the diagram your team developed to help explain the principles involved and the appearance of the device. After each group has presented its work, compliment each other on the presentation.

Exercise 3 Now that you have listened to others giving and receiving compliments and have practiced doing so yourself, you will probably be more aware of the fine points of this skill in everyday encounters. For the next day or two, pay particular attention to any giving or receiving of compliments that you either participate in or overhear. Note the circumstances, the relationship of the people involved, their attitudes, and the particular expressions used. Were there any instances in which you thought the compliments or the protests on receiving them were overdone? Were there any expressions used that were new to you? How many compliments did you give in one day? How many did you receive? Do you think that being a self-conscious observer of giving and receiving compliments caused you to give more compliments, fewer compliments, or had no effect on the number of compliments you gave? Share your observations and answers with your classmates.

Exercise 4 Try this activity just for fun. Take turns buttering each other up—that is, giving an excessive number of compliments because you want something and don't want your request to be refused. You may want to role-play one or more of the following situations for this activity, or you may choose just to be yourselves.

Suggested Situations

1. a Hollywood party with producers, directors, actors, and actresses
2. a company Christmas party
3. a reception for a famous visiting physicist
4. a reception at the White House
5. a dinner party with your future in-laws

CHAPTER 11
MEDICINE

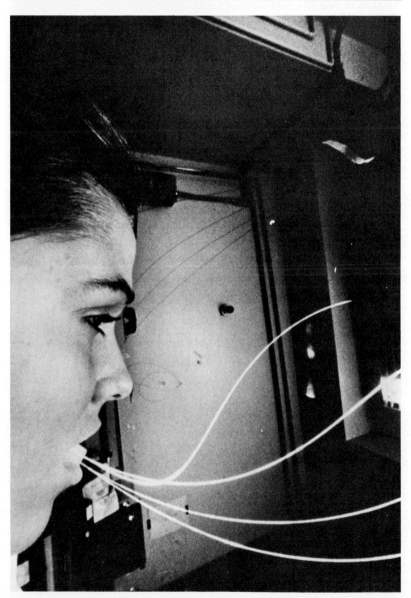

Laser treatment for cancer of the mouth.

The science fiction creations of the 1940s and '50s are rapidly becoming realities of the 1980s. Space satellites orbit the earth, wrist radios and televisions are available through mail-order catalogs, and jet-propelled backpacks can be obtained for the right price. Space-age technology has turned fantasies into realities and has gone beyond fantasy to make the unimaginable real. Even the infamous "death ray" has already been developed. Fortunately, thus far many people have seen fit to turn the awesome powers of this ray to beneficial purposes. The lecture in this chapter deals with its use in the field of medicine.

Lecture: Laser Technology and Medicine
Skill A: Predicting Exam Questions
Skill B: Acquiescing and Expressing Reservations

PART ONE

DISCUSSION

As a class, discuss the following:

1. Compare what you may know (or imagine) about medical practices and surgery in the 1880s with medical practices and surgery in the 1980s.

2. Consider medical advances occurring in the last twenty-five years that have benefited friends, relatives, or acquaintances of yours. Describe the person's medical problem and how a particular medical advance benefited that person.

3. What comes to mind when you hear the word *laser?* Describe all the ways you know of that lasers are used. Have you or anyone you've known ever seen a laser in operation? If so, describe the experience to the class.

VOCABULARY

To figure out the following secret phrase, fill in the blanks of the puzzle with the correct form of the words from the vocabulary list. Then find the letters to fill in the secret phrase by matching the numbers underneath. Or if you think you know the secret phrase already, write it in the blanks and use those letters to help you figure out the rest of the puzzle.

Secret Phrase

Clue: This is Albert Einstein's definition of science.

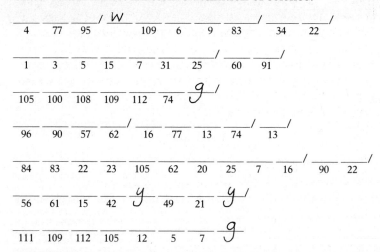

___ ___ ___ / W ___ ___ ___ ___ ___ / ___ ___ /
4 77 95   109 6 9 83   34 22

___ ___ ___ ___ ___ ___ ___ / ___ ___ /
1 3 5 15 7 31 25   60 91

___ ___ ___ ___ ___ ___ ___ g /
105 100 108 109 112 74

___ ___ ___ ___ / ___ ___ ___ ___ / ___ /
96 90 57 62   16 77 13 74   13

___ ___ ___ ___ ___ ___ ___ ___ ___ ___ / ___ ___ /
84 83 22 23 105 62 20 25 7 16   90 22

___ ___ ___ ___ y ___ ___ y /
56 61 15 42   49 21

___ ___ ___ ___ ___ ___ ___ g
111 109 112 105 12 5 7

Fill in the blanks that follow with the correct forms of these words and phrases:

blockage
blood clots
cholesterol deposits
to emit
fiber-optic

local anesthetic
postoperative complications
to rupture
suction
trauma

a. ___ ___ ___ ___ ___ ___ ___
      1   2   3   4   5   6   7

b. ___ ___ ___ ___ ___ ___ ___ ___
      8   9   10 11 12 13 14 15

c. ___ ___ ___ ___ ___ ___
      16 17 18 19 20 21

d. ___ ___ ___ ___ ___   ___ ___ ___ ___ ___
      22 23 24 25 26   27 28 29 30 31

e. ___ ___ ___ ___ ___ / ___ ___ ___ ___ ___
      32 33 34 35 36   37 38 39 40 41

f. ___ ___ ___ ___ ___ ___ ___ ___
      42 43 44 45 46 47 48 49

g. ___ ___ ___ ___ ___ ___ ___ ___ ___ ___ ___ ___ ___ /
      50 51 52 53 54 55 56 57 58 59 60 61 62

      ___ ___ ___ ___ ___ ___ ___ ___ ___ ___ ___ ___ ___
      63 64 65 66 67 68 69 70 71 72 73 74 75

h. ___ ___ ___ ___ ___ ___ ___ ___ ___ ___ ___ /
      76 77 78 79 80 81 82 83 84 85 86

      ___ ___ ___ ___ ___ ___ ___ ___
      87 88 89 90 91 92 93 94

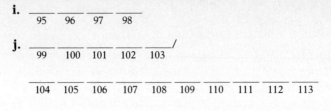

i. ___ ___ ___ ___
  95 96 97 98

j. ___ ___ ___ ___ ___/
  99 100 101 102 103

___ ___ ___ ___ ___ ___ ___ ___ ___ ___
104 105 106 107 108 109 110 111 112 113

___ ___ ___ ___ ___ ___ ___ ___ ___ ___

Clues

a. pulling or sucking in (caused by creating differences in air pressure between interior or exterior space)

b. something that causes closure; an obstruction

c. severe injury to the body

d. referring to a threadlike tool that helps doctors see into the body without cutting it open

e. semisolid masses of the fluid that circulate in the arteries and veins

f. broken or burst open

g. medical problems arising after an operation

h. lumps of a fatlike substance that can cause blockage in the arteries

i. to give out or send forth

j. a substance that produces insensitivity to pain in the area where it is injected

PART TWO

SKILL A: PREDICTING EXAM QUESTIONS

Although good grades may not always reflect deep understanding of a subject, they are the basis for academic advancement, and therefore most students are concerned about getting good grades. One of the strategies for getting good grades on an exam is to determine what questions the instructor is likely to ask. One way to do this is to listen attentively for hints that the instructor might give, either intentionally or unintentionally, during lectures. Obviously, any information the instructor repeats from readings in your textbook is very likely to appear on an exam. Another hint is that instructors often slow down their speech or raise their voices when they consider material important. Sometimes a lecturer will state specifically that the material being discussed is likely to be on an exam.

Facts obviously are good candidates for exam questions. In a course about the history of medicine, for example, the question Who performed the first laser surgery? is a reasonable one. In an engineering course, Who developed the laser? would be a more likely question.

Any information about recent research, especially the instructor's own, is likely to be used on exams. One reason for this, of course, is that most instructors want to make sure their students' knowledge is up-to-date. A second reason is that some instructors like to know if students have been attending lectures. They can determine this readily by asking exam questions on unpublished research that was described in class and cannot be looked up in the library. Last, but certainly not least, any information the lecturer presents in a handout is fair game for an exam question.

Listen In

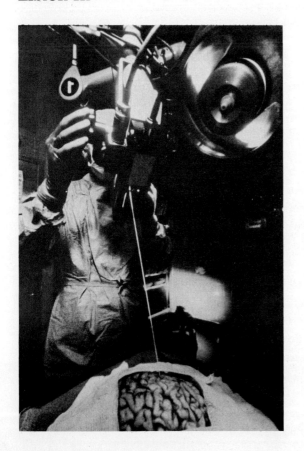

CO_2 argon/lasers can be used to vaporize brain tumors.

Lecture 11: Laser Technology and Medicine

1. Laser = Light Amplification by Stimulated Emission of Radiation

2. Types of lasers used in surgery
    a. YAG = yttrium-aluminum garnet laser: uses a synthetic gemstone
       as a conductor to produce the laser energy
    b. CO_2 laser: uses carbon dioxide gas
    c. argon laser: uses argon gas
    d. HeNe laser: uses a mixture of helium and nitrogen gases

3. Two laser-assisted surgical processes

    a. photocoagulation necrosis: cuts, burns, or fuses all tissues
       in its path
    b. photoradiation therapy: uses laser in combination with the
       drug HpD; destroys only selected tissues (e.g., cancer cells)

4. Instruments used in combination with lasers to perform surgery
    a. X rays
    b. fiber optics

5. Type of operation determines type of laser to be used

    a. argon laser, selectively absorbed by tissues and can be
       passed through fiber optics; therefore used for surgery
       such as:
            relairing small ruptured blood vessels
            reattaching detached retinas
            removing tattoos and birthmarks
    b. YAG laser, not selectively absorbed by tissue and can be passed
       through fiber optics; therefore good for:
            penetrating blood clots
            repairing large ruptured blood vessels
            reducing the size of tumors
    c. Carbon dioxide laser, cannot easily be passed through fiber
       optics but is still favored for:
            surgical procedures the ears,
            nose, and mouth
            nose, and mouth
            delicate neurological,
            gynecological, and burn surgery

Argon laser being used in surgery on a human ear.

Engineering 203   **HANDOUT 2**

Lecture 11: Laser Technology and Medicine

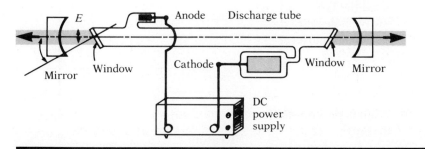

He-Ne laser configuration.

Exercise 1   The lecture in this chapter, "Laser Technology and Medicine," might be for an engineering course in which the instructor is interested in applications of technical advances in engineering to everyday life. Imagine this: One student, Jeffrey, who heard this lecture and has been practicing predicting exam questions, wrote down the five questions that follow. How accurate do you think his predictions are? Listen to the lecture as many times as necessary for you to judge this. If you believe Jeffrey is right—that the question is likely to be on an exam—circle *yes*. If you think Jeffrey is wrong and the question is not likely to be on an exam, circle *no*. If you can, make a note about your reasons for circling *yes* or *no*.

Example: The laser is becoming a more and more popular surgical tool. True or false?

Good Question?

Yes (No)

Reason: _too general, too easy_

_____

_____

1. What does the acronym *laser* stand for?

Yes   No

Reason: _____

_____

_____

_____

2. How much do lasers cost?

Yes   No

Reason: _____

_____

_____

3. Which hospital recently used the laser to clear away cholesterol deposits in an artery?

Yes   No

Reason: _____

_____

_____

_____

4. What is photoradiation therapy?

Yes   No

Reason: _____

_____

_____

_____

5. What precautions are necessary during laser surgery?

Yes   No

Reason: _____

_____

_____

_____

Exercise 2   Listen to the lecture again. This time, take notes. As you take notes, consider what information the instructor would be most likely to select for exam questions. Put an asterisk (*), N.B. (*nota bene* in Latin, meaning "note well"), or some other indicator next to that information as a reminder that while you listened to the lecture you thought the instructor would probably test you on this bit of information.

Examples: *Most lasers use CO_2, Ar, or a mixture of He Ne.*

N.B. Most lasers use CO_2, Ar, or a mixture of He Ne.

Speak Out

Exercise 1   As a class, discuss the types of exam questions instructors ask (for example, true/false, multiple-choice, short answer, and essay). Then discuss how the subject area of a course (for example, electrical engineering, history, philosophy, urban planning) may influence the kind of question the instructor chooses. For instance, when might a literature instructor choose to ask a true/false question? When might an engineering instructor choose to ask an essay question? In your discussion, consider the kinds of questions that would be asked in courses such as the following or any additional courses you care to bring up:

biology
chemistry
computer science
engineering
English
history
marketing
operations research
philosophy
statistics
urban planning

Exercise 2   Based on your notes on the lecture, ask a classmate at least ten questions you think might appear on an exam. After your partner has answered your questions, answer his or her questions. Discuss whether you think these questions would actually appear on an exam. Then change partners and try the activ-again. Do this a few more times, if time permits. As a class, discuss the variety of types of questions you and your classmates predicted would be on an exam.

SKILL B: ACQUIESCING AND EXPRESSING RESERVATIONS

A common feeling people have when dealing with professionals such as doctors is one of yielding, of being obliging or submissive. Many times they become angry or frustrated with themselves because they didn't speak up enough in the presence of a professional when they had a question that was troubling them. Professionals often try to project an image that they are much wiser than their patients or clients are and that they know all the answers. And this image sometimes makes people lose sight of what is in their own best interest. But remember that professionals of all types, and doctors specifically, are as fallible as anyone else and do make mistakes that can be costly to the patient.

You may trust your doctor completely and wish to accept or acquiesce to his or her suggestions. But sometimes you may have some reservations about what your doctor is suggesting. For example, you should speak up when you think your doctor has overlooked something in his or her diagnosis or wants to try a treatment that is not essential or that has some risk attached to it. Here are some expressions you might find useful in these two instances.

Acquiescing /əkwɪ'ɛs/ agree.

Do whatever you need to do.
I'm putting myself completely in your hands.
I suppose you must know best.
I trust you completely.
If you think that's best.
Whatever you say.

Expressing reservations

Let me think it over.
How long do I have to think it over?
I'd like to get a second opinion.
One drawback is . . .
Possibly, but . . .
Yes, but the question really is . . .
What bothers me is . . .
What I'm afraid of is . . .

Listen to the following conversations, which have examples of people acquiescing and expressing reservations. Compare the way the patients handle the situations.

Conversation 1

Doctor: The hospital has just purchased a new laser machine. I think it would be the perfect treatment for your condition.

Patient: Those newfangled things kinda' scare me. Are you sure they're safe?

Doctor: We have some of the finest technicians in the world here. No one can do it better than we can.

Patient: Yes, I know everyone here has a very good reputation and everyone has been so nice to me, but this is a big step. What happens if something goes wrong?

Doctor: Let me assure you that you are receiving the best medical care available anywhere in the world. The chances of something going wrong are almost nonexistent. This same treatment has saved hundreds of lives.

Patient: Well, I suppose you must know best.

Conversation 2

Doctor: The hospital just purchased a new laser machine, and I think it would be the perfect treatment for your condition.

Patient: Perhaps, but I really don't know anything about it.

Doctor: Most people don't; it's so new. Now I suggest . . .

Patient: Excuse me, Dr. Jones, but I really do feel I should know what I'm getting into before doing this. Do you have any literature on laser-assisted operations?

Doctor: Well, not on hand, but why don't you leave it up to me to decide what's best?

Patient: I'm really not questioning your judgment, but I need to be certain for myself what the risks are.

Doctor: You certainly have that right, but I think you are wasting your time. The medical literature available is difficult for a layman to read, and besides, your condition could become very serious soon.

Patient: How long do I have to think it over?

Doctor: Two to three weeks at most.

Patient: That seems enough time to do some research, and I'd like to get a second opinion. I want to be 100 percent sure before I go ahead.

Listen In

Exercise 1   Listen to the lecture. After every major operation is described, decide how you would respond if you were to undergo it. Discuss with your classmates what reservations you would have and how you would verbalize them to your doctor. How would you feel if the operation involved some risks, but it was described to you as "the only way"? Would you seek alternative forms of treatment?

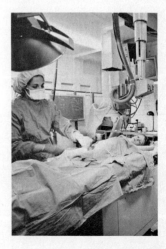

Exercise 2   Listen to the conversations again. Which expressions did each patient use to acquiesce? To express reservations? Was there anything else the patients did to indicate acquiescence or to express reservations? Any particular questions, statements, or tone of voice? Share your responses with your classmates.

Speak Out

One ethical question involved in physician/patient relationships is whether physicians have the right to withhold information from patients or to make decisions for them based on what they believe is best. With a partner, role-play one of the following situations involving doctors and patients. Decide how the patient should respond to the doctor. If time permits, try another role-play with this partner, or you may wish to change partners to role-play the same situation or another one. Then ask volunteers representing each of the scenarios to present their role-plays to the whole class.

1. Sam, forty-four years old, has an excellent reputation in the community as a father, a good provider, and a concerned citizen. He is president of one of his city's leading banks, and he generously donates his time to a number of local charities. His doctor, a close friend for many years, has just given Sam a yearly checkup and found, to his horror, that Sam has an irreversible and fatal form of pancreatic cancer that will kill him in six months. Chemotherapy would not be effective, so the doctor doesn't even suggest it. But he is puzzled about what to do. If he tells Sam about his condition, he is afraid Sam will "fall apart" and his remaining time will be torture for him and those around him. He has seen this happen before. Therefore, he decides not to tell Sam about his condition.

2. Marcia, thirty-eight, is a single parent with three small children. Lately she has suffered severe mood swings. She cries for hours over small irritations and has suffered from severe headaches for months. She might have a brain tumor, but her doctor is not sure. He suggests an exploratory operation to find out.

3. Kamal has been sick for quite some time. He is in a foreign country and goes to a doctor who is highly recommended by the student health service at the university. She tells him that his kidneys are failing and that he must be hospitalized immediately and must receive a kidney transplant as soon as possible.

CHAPTER 12
THE FUTURE

When you think of the future, what do you think of? Living a long time? Of marriage, perhaps? Of children, grandchildren, and great-grandchildren? Of a good job? Of world peace and prosperity? Or is your vision of the world much darker? For instance, do you fear bringing children into a world where natural resources such as forests, oil, water, and air are rapidly being used up? Have you given up on the notion of world peace and prosperity because of reports of overpopulation and the prospect of world famine? The lecture in this chapter presents predictions made by a presidential commission on what the world will be like in the year 2000.

Lecture: The World in the Year 2000

Skill A: Critical Thinking

Skill B: Speculating about the Future/Reminiscing about the Past

PART ONE

DISCUSSION

As a class or in small groups, discuss the following:

Exercise 1   Imagine for the next few moments that two decades or so have gone by and it is now the year 2010. For you, it is an ideal world; all your hopes for yourself and humanity have been realized. Take a moment to let this image of an ideal world sink in and then share your responses to these questions.

1. How old are you?
2. What kind of job do you have?
3. Where do you live?
4. What do you see when you look out the window at home? At work?
5. Is there romance in your life?
6. What do you do during your leisure time?
7. What do you do on vacations?
8. In what ways are you involved in community or government affairs?
9. What are your friends like?
10. What is a typical day like for you?

Exercise 2 You may feel that the ideal world you've been describing is not really a possibility. You may even fear that you and the rest of humanity face a dark future. What are some of your worst fears for the future? Share these with your classmates. Then consider together how each of these fears arose and why. For instance, is the source of the fear a program you saw on t.v.? A movie? An article in a newspaper or magazine? Is the source something a friend, acquaintance, or family member said to you?

Now try to determine if these fears are reasonable. Are they based on hard evidence such as statistics or scientific surveys, or are they based on things such as feelings, opinions, or gossip? Do you think you have enough hard evidence about any of your fears to persuade a government body to do something?

VOCABULARY

The definitions of the words in this list reflect the ways in which they are used in the lecture in this chapter.

apathy   indifference, lack of care, interest, or emotion

to commission   to authorize, command, empower

to deplete   to use up

extinct   no longer existing (refers to a group or class, not to an individual)

to implement   to put into action

inflation   the decrease in the worth of paper money as more and more of it is printed

to replenish   to replace or restore

scarcity   shortage

to have strings attached   to have obligations, often not formalized, beyond a basic agreement

Each of the incomplete analogies in the items that follow contains one vocabulary word (or phrase) from the list. Read the items and fill in the blank with a word or group of words to complete the analogy. Compare your answers with your classmates'.

Example: polar bear : living :: _dinosaur_____ : extinct
(Read: "*Polar bear* is to *living* as *dinosaur* is to *extinct*.")

1. add : subtract :: _____ : deplete

2. present : absent :: _____ : apathy

3. fish in the sea : plenty :: _____ : scarcity

4. to lose weight : to gain weight :: _____ : replenish

5. rising prices : _____ :: hard economic times : depression

6. zoo animal: wild animal :: to have strings attached : _____

7. red light: green light :: _____ : commission

8. make: recipe :: implement: _____

PART TWO

SKILL A: CRITICAL THINKING

You cannot really memorize rules for critical thinking as you might memorize rules in the study of grammar. Critical thinking involves evaluating facts or opinions and making your own decisions, rather than blindly accepting what you are told.

Making accurate analyses is not always easy however. Sometimes people hold on to irrational beliefs and are afraid of changing. This can lead to prejudice and narrow-mindedness. Other times people are uninformed or misinformed. Effective critical thinking involves withholding judgment and stepping back to view things objectively, and it involves mindful deliberation.

Throughout this book, you have been introduced to patterns of logic that can help you develop your ability to think critically. As you consider a speaker's ideas, you can, for example, compare and contrast your ideas or another's with the speaker's (Chapter 6). And seeing cause-and-effect relationships (Chapter 7) may help you break down complicated ideas into a simpler sequence of events and results. Critical thinking (and listening) also requires that you distinguish facts and opinions (Chapter 9). Using these skills will help you refine your critical thinking ability. As you refine this ability, you will find that material presented to you generally falls into one of three categories.

1. *Facts.* Facts can be proved either right or wrong by comparing them with accurate data.

2. *Questionable concepts.* Vague terms and abstract ideas can be defined or stated in different ways. You accept or reject a certain speaker's interpretation based on your assessment.

3. *Opinions.* Someone's judgment, beliefs, values, or tastes can be agreed or disagreed with. For example, consider the following:

Gerard O'Neill, author and scientist, has seriously considered the idea of colonies in space. He believes that by the year 2010 it will be technically feasible to build a space city in the shape of a cylinder that would rotate through space. O'Neill is convinced that such colonies would provide an adequate alternative to life on earth for our ever-expanding population. Fiber-optic light would duplicate the passing of the sun overhead, so people would continue to function in the daytime and nighttime they are used to. These space citizens would live in a cylinder, and their view up would be of other people and buildings standing upside down. This would be the most serious drawback: The sky would be missing.

What are the facts in this passage? In general, names and numbers can be checked for accuracy, so they are either true or false, facts or untruths. The name of the scientist could be considered a fact; you can prove it's his name. The technical elements are also facts; fiber optics could be used to attempt to simulate the sun.

What questionable concepts can you find? First, who has determined the technical feasibility? Do *all* the experts agree with O'Neill? And how closely will the lighting actually resemble the sun?

Lastly, what are the opinions in this illustration? O'Neill believes that space colonies provide a solution practical enough to consider seriously, but how do other scientists feel? How do *you* feel?

To evaluate an opinion like O'Neill's, or any other value statement, you may want to ask yourself these questions:

1. Is the speaker using emotion rather than logic to persuade me?
2. Is an issue being oversimplified or misconstrued?
3. Is irrelevant material used?
4. Is the speaker basing his or her ideas on valid proven theory?

Also, you should examine how your own biases may be affecting your acceptance or rejection of something. An American writer, Ralph Waldo Emerson, once wrote: "What can we see, read, acquire, but ourselves? Take the book, my friend, and read your eyes out, you will never find there what I find." In other words, each person is unique and will respond differently to what he or she reads and hears. But to be critical thinkers, we must avoid allowing individual responses to cloud our understanding of the speaker's message. We must first hear the core meaning of the speaker without judgment. Then we must carefully evaluate what we have heard.

In summary, here are a few do's and don't's to guide your critical thinking:

1. Don't believe everything you hear. Be skeptical.

2. Question not only the controversial but the seemingly plausible concepts as well.

3. Find out the speaker's attitude and purpose. Does the speaker have a bias? Is he or she being paid to support a specific concept? Are important points of an argument left out so as to "weight" the argument in favor of one side?

4. Look for inconsistencies, so that you are not fooled by arguments based on poor reasoning.

5. Examine data to ensure that the speaker has presented it accurately and that you are interpreting it correctly.

Listen In

Exercise 1   Numerous facts, concepts, and statements of opinion are presented in this chapter's lecture. Listen to the lecture once through. Then listen once or twice again and write down at least four statements of fact (in which the definition of terms is generally not argued), four statements of concepts (in which the definition of terms is debatable), and four statements of opinion (personal values). Analyze these statements according to the criteria in "Skill A." Share these statements and your answers to the following questions with your classmates.

In the year 2000, will our planet be able to accommodate a population that seems to be increasing geometrically?

Family planning is fast
becoming a worldwide
concern.

1. Do you think the statements of fact hold up on closer exami-
   nation? Why or why not?

2. Do you agree with the ways in which the speaker uses terms in
   the statements of concepts? Why or why not? Do you agree with
   the speaker's opinions? Why or why not?

3. Do you think that the speaker is trying to persuade you to
   accept a particular point of view? If so, which one? What are the
   techniques the speaker uses to do this?

Exercise 2   The lecturer presents several possible remedies for
the world's ills. Listen to the lecture again, noting in particular these
proposals. Share your list of proposals with your classmates and
evaluate them by asking the questions presented in "Skill A." For
example, What assumptions lie behind the proposals? or, What is
the motivation of the speaker in presenting these proposals?

_____

_____

_____

_____

_____

Speak Out

Exercise 1 The best way to learn critical thinking is to apply it in everyday life. Break into discussion groups and assign each member the task of collecting things people say or write about the future. Do this in any of the following ways:

1. Interview at least six people (friends, relatives, strangers) about the future. You might first design a questionnaire with your classmates including five to ten items such as the following:

    a. What do you think life will be like in the year 2000 or 2100?
    b. Do you think the future will be better than the present? Why or why not?

    Then describe and discuss with your classmates the kinds of assumptions the people you interviewed made. Do you think they are valid assumptions?

2. Bring in newspaper articles or books that contain material about the future. The study of the future may be called *futurology* in your bookstore or library.

3. Find any picture or advertisement that is intended to show life in the future. What is it based on? How realistic do you think it is? Why was it displayed where it was?

In your discussion groups, evaluate the information you collected.

Exercise 2 For further practice of critical thinking skills, discuss with your classmates as many of the following statements as time permits. Do you agree or disagree with the statement(s)? Why or why not? Do you agree or disagree with your classmates regarding the validity of the statement(s)? Do you agree with your classmates on the definitions of the terms, especially the more abstract concepts?

1. All people are born equal.
2. The United States was a democracy before women were allowed to vote.
3. Animals think.
4. Morality is irrelevant to someone living alone on an island.
5. You are not responsible for what happens to others.
6. Alcoholism is a disease.
7. Virtue is its own reward.

SKILL B: SPECULATING ABOUT THE FUTURE, REMINISCING ABOUT THE PAST

Dealing with the unexpected is part of being alive, and although some unexpected events turn out to be pleasant surprises, most people like to prepare themselves for what is to come. Since most people are not clairvoyant and cannot see exactly what will happen in the future, they tend to prepare themselves for future events by speculating about various possibilities. And whether they engage in speculation about universally significant issues such as life on earth in the year 2000 or about daily events such as the chance of rain, they often use one of the following expressions to introduce a speculation:

I have a hunch that . . .
I'd guess (speculate) that . . .
I wouldn't be surprised if . . .
I'll bet that . . .
It is doubtful that . . .
It is inevitable that . . .
. . . is bound to . . .
My guess is that . . .
My projection is that . . .
There's a good chance that . . .
There's no chance that . . .
There's not much chance that . . .

Inevitably, some possibilities of the future become events of the past. You may want to hold onto precious moments and make them last forever but the best you can do is store them away in your memory to enjoy again and again in later years. Or you may wish that certain terrible events would end quickly. Eventually they do end, but you are left with indelible images stored in your memory that inevitably call up intense emotion when brought to mind. The two extremes of precious moments and terrible events and the many other events in between are there in your memory, waiting for you to call them up. Perhaps someone asks you a question about a past event or says something that reminds you of an incident in the past that you decide is relevant to the present conversation. Then you will want to share your recollections, your reminiscences, and the following expressions will be useful:

As I recall . . .
As I remember it . . .
I'll never forget the time . . .
(Do you) Remember the time. . . ?

In those days . . .
My recollection is that . .
That reminds me of the time . . .

Listen to the following conversation, in which two speakers are speculating and reminiscing:

A: Good morning.

B: Good morning. And how are you today?

A: I didn't sleep too well and I feel a bit tired, but I'm really eager to get home. . . . Well, let's get back to work. Where were we? As I recall, before I went to sleep, you were working on the calculations for our time of arrival.

B: That's right. You've been asleep exactly three years, twenty-one days, five hours, and ten minutes.

A: Now, now—no need to be sarcastic. Just tell me when we'll arrive home on earth, will you?

B: Well, my guess is that we'll arrive at the spaceport in Dallas on February 23, 2147.

A: Your guess? You're supposed to *know* these things. And where did you learn that expression, anyway?

B: Same place you did, of course. Back on earth. And you know as well as I do that some of our instruments were not functioning for a while. We could only speculate how long they were off; so based on speculation, I can only guess our time of arrival. But don't worry, there's a good chance we'll arrive in February, as I said.

A: Swell—this reminds me of the time you broke down and miscalculated all of the readings from the instruments. I'm surprised we got home at all that time.

B: Well, that's not the case this time! I assure you I'm perfectly fine.

A: Okay, okay—well, anyway, it will be good to get home.

B: But don't be surprised if things are a lot different now. There's a good chance that Dallas will seem almost foreign to you.

A: Yeah—I'll never forget the time we took our first trip. What a jolt that was, arriving home and everyone was ten years older. The clothing styles, the music—everything was different.

B: Mmm. That takes me back to when you first decided to become a space pilot.

A: What? How do you know about that?

B: I know everything you know. Remember the time you and Salina Gravitz went to that party in Chicago and then . . .

A: Enough reminiscing! If you don't quit doing that, I have a hunch that a computer I know quite well is going to have its circuits rearranged!

B: Oh, all right! But don't forget, it's bound to be lonely out here without me to talk to.

reminising

*have a hunch
(feeling).*

The future: A drought-stricken area in Africa or irrigated farmlands in New Mexico.

Listen In

Exercise 1   In the lecture in this chapter the speaker speculates about what the world will be like in the year 2000. Listen to the lecture again. Each time the speaker makes a statement that is or could have been introduced by one of the expressions used for speculating, write down a possible expression and the statement. (The lecturer uses other expressions for speculating besides those listed in "Skill B.") In response to these speculations, you may wish to make a few of your own. The following speculations have been taken from the lecture to get you started.

	Lecturer's Opinion	**Your Speculation**
1. _____	The gap between the wealthy industrialized countries and the developing countries will continue to widen.	Do you agree? Explain. _____ _____ _____
2. _____	The loss of forests will lead to the loss of topsoil. Without trees to hold the soil in place, there will be more deserts.	How will this change the earth? _____ _____ _____ _____

183

	Lecturer's Opinion	Your Speculation
3. _____	For many nations, starvation will become an even greater problem as the year 2000 approaches.	Do you believe this? Explain. _____ _____ _____ _____
4. _____	The United States, with its relatively stable economy, might lead a global program of providing food.	Is this realistic? _____ _____ _____
5. _____	Exports should be priced according to the incomes of the consumer nations.	Why won't this happen? _____ _____ _____
6. _____	"The only limit to our realization of tomorrow will be our doubt of today."	What does this mean? _____ _____ _____

Compare your answers with your classmates'.

Exercise 2 Listen to the conversation again and answer these questions.

1. What does Speaker A speculate about? _____

    Speaker B? _____

2. What does Speaker A reminisce about? _____

    Speaker B? _____

3. Who is Speaker A? _____

    Speaker B? _____

4. Why does Speaker A want Speaker B to stop reminiscing?

_____

_____

Speak Out

Exercise 1   Are you wondering what the future will bring? Why not visit the local psychic or fortune teller? In groups of three to five, take turns playing the role of a psychic or fortune teller who "sees all, knows all, and tells all." Let your classmates ask you whatever questions come to mind about future global or personal events. As you answer each of their questions, use an expression listed in "Skill B" to introduce your speculation about the future.

Exercise 2   Reunions are popular in many cultures. Officially, there are family reunions, class reunions, and team reunions, to name a few. But any gathering of friends who have not seen each other for a long time can be called a reunion.
   Imagine that you and your classmates have decided to come back together for a reunion. At a party, you are getting reacquainted by sharing what has happened in the last twenty-five years, reminiscing about the past, and speculating about the future. Throughout the activity, try to stay in character and play yourself as you might be twenty-five years from now. If possible, you might want to have some refreshments at your reunion party to get you into the mood.

Exercise 3   Divide the class into four groups to represent four generations of a family, which will include great-grandparents and great-grandchildren. Then decide what your individual roles will be and imagine that you are all attending a family reunion. It's like most other family reunions, except for one thing—it is taking place in the year 2100. Share your reminiscences and speculations with the members of your family.

Scoring for Risk-Taker Test, Pages 27–28

Question	Strong yes	Weak yes	maybe	Weak no	Strong no
1.	4	3	2	1	0
2.	6	5	3	2	1
3.	5	4	3	2	1
4.	6	5	3	2	1
5.	7	6	4	2	1
6.	2	1	.5	0	0
7.	3	2	1	.5	0
8.	6	5	3	2	1
9.	7	6	4	2	1
10.	7	6	4	2	1
11.	9	8	6	4	2
12.	7	6	4	2	1
13.	10	9	8	4	2
14.	8	7	5	3	1
15.	10	9	8	4	2
16.	10	9	8	4	2
17.	5	4	2	1	0
18.	4	3	2	1	0
19.	5	4	2	1	0
20.	9	8	6	4	2
21.	8	7	5	3	1
22.	7	6	4	2	1
23.	3	2	1	.5	0
24.	2	1	.5	0	0
25.	7	6	4	2	1

Crossword Solutions, from Page 131

				¹B							⁴A						²I
				O		³A	C	C	O	M	P	A	N	I	M	E	N	T
				O							C					D
			⁵S	E	G	R	E	G	A	T	I	O	N				I
				D							U					F
					⁶C	E	N	S	O	R	S	H	I	P		F
		⁷O								T					E
		U				⁸R	⁹E	A	F	F	I	R	M		R
		T		¹⁰B		N				C		¹¹B		E
		R		L		H	¹²H				A		N
¹³H		A		U		A	I				C		T
A		G		E		N	L				K
R		E	¹⁴M	U	S	I	C	O	L	O	G	I	S	T
M		O				E	B				R
O		U					I				A
¹⁵N	O	S	T	A	L	G	I	C	A	L	L	Y		C
I							L				K
¹⁶C	E	L	L	I	S	T		Y			E
S											D

187